W9-CKT-740

Lorette Wilmot Library
Nazareth College of Rochester

DEMCO

Nursing & Philanthropy

an energizing metaphor for the 21st century

CONFERENCE PROCEEDINGS

Compiled by Angela Barron McBride

WITHDRAWN
LORETTE WILMOT LIBRARY
NAZARETH COLLEGE

Sigma Theta Tau International

Publishing Director: Jeff Burnham
Book Acquisitions Editor: Fay L. Bower, DNSc, FAAN
Proofreader: Linda Canter

Copyright© 2000 by Sigma Theta Tau International

All rights reserved. This book is protected by copyright. No part of it may
be reproduced, stored in a retrieval system, or transmitted in any form or
by any means, electronic, mechanical, photocopying, recording, or
otherwise, without written permission from the publisher.

Printed in the United States of America
Composition by Sigma Theta Tau International
Designed by Bruce L. Williams

Sigma Theta Tau International Honor Society of Nursing
550 West North Street
Indianapolis, IN 46202
For additional titles, visit our Web site: www.nursingsociety.org/publications

ISBN: 1-930538-02-2

03 04 05 /9 8 7 6 5 4 3 2

Contents

Chapter 1

Yesterday, Today and Tomorrow
Helen K. Grace and Gloria R. Smith

Chapter 2

Sara T. Fry

Chapter 3

Sharon Farley

Chapter 4

Robyn Gibboney

Chapter 5

What Is the Philanthropic Appeal
Joyce J. Fitzpatrick

Preface

A national invitational conference on "Nursing and Philanthropy: An Energizing Metaphor for the 21st Century" took place on December 1-2, 1997. The meeting was sponsored by Indiana University School of Nursing and the Indiana University Center on Philanthropy in association with Sigma Theta Tau International, particularly Alpha Chapter, and the Association for Research on Nonprofit Organizations and Voluntary Action (ARNOVA). The timing of the meeting took advantage of the fact that Sigma Theta Tau International was hosting its biennial convention and ARNOVA was holding its annual meeting, both in Indianapolis within the same week. The juxtaposition of these two major events provided an opportunity for partnership between two major fields, nursing and philanthropy, for the purpose of exploring common concerns and shared values.

It is particularly appropriate that Sigma Theta Tau International's Center Nursing Press is publishing the resulting proceedings for a variety of reasons. Sigma Theta Tau International, nursing's honor society, was founded in 1922 at Indiana University (IU). It went on to become the first nursing organization to mount a major fund-raising campaign when it built its headquarters building in 1989 on IU's Indianapolis campus. The Indiana University Center on Philanthropy was founded in the late 1980s, and subsequently rented office space on the third floor of that new building. In December 1997, Sigma Theta Tau International was celebrating the 75th anniversary of its founding, and the conclusion of its second major fund-raising campaign. In one decade, the association had not only mounted two successful campaigns, but it had convinced many nurses to become philanthropists and many philanthropists to invest in the nursing profession.

Acknowledgments

Many individuals contributed to this invitational conference, and thus to this manuscript. A complete list of speakers and respondents can be found on the following page. Special thanks are due, however, to Robyn Gibboney and Warren Ilchman for their leadership roles in conceptualizing and organizing this meeting. The Lilly Foundation, through a program grant to the IU Center on Philanthropy, and the Helene Fuld Foundation both contributed significantly to the support of this conference. Finally, this monograph is dedicated to Nell J. Watts, the first full-time executive officer of Sigma Theta Tau International, and Linda Brimmer, the first development officer of that organization, for their visionary roles in the development of the link between nursing and philanthropy.

Angela Barron McBride, RN, PhD, FAAN
Past President, Sigma Theta Tau International (1987-89)
University Dean, Indiana University School of Nursing

Participants

(Nursing and Philanthropy Conference December 1997)

PRESENTERS: Sharon Farley, Executive Associate Dean, Indiana University School of Nursing; Joyce Fitzpatrick, Dean, Frances Payne Bolton School Nursing, Case Western Reserve University, and President-Elect, American Academy of Nursing; Sara Fry, Professor of Nursing Ethics, Boston College School of Nursing; Robyn Gibboney, Director of Development, Indiana University School of Nursing; Helen Grace, Special Assistant to the President, W. K. Kellogg Foundation; Warren Ilchman, Executive Director, Indiana University Center on Philanthropy; Angela Barron McBride, Distinguished Professor and University Dean, Indiana University School of Nursing; Robert Payton, Professor of Philanthropic Studies and Founding Executive Director, Indiana University Center on Philanthropy. **RESPONDENTS:** Anne Belcher, Assistant Professor, Indiana University School of Nursing; Robert Bringle, Director, Indiana University - Purdue University Indianapolis (IUPUI) Office of Service Learning; Anne Donchin, Professor of Philosophy, Indiana University - Purdue University Indianapolis (IUPUI); Vernice Ferguson, Senior Fellow Emeritus, University of Pennsylvania School of Nursing, and Former Chief of Nursing, Veterans Administration; Ken Gladish, Executive Director, The Indianapolis Foundation; George D. Lundberg, Editor, Journal of the American Medical Association; Beverly Malone, President, American Nurses Association; Angela Barron McBride, Distinguished Professor and University Dean, Indiana University School of Nursing; Paula Parker-Sawyers, Executive Director, Association of Black Foundation Executives and member, Program Staff at the IU Center on Philanthropy; Edward Queen, Visiting Professor of Religion, Indiana University Center on Philanthropy; Jane Schultz, Associate Professor, Women's Studies, Indiana University - Purdue University Indianapolis (IUPUI); Eugene Temple, Vice Chancellor for External Affairs, Indiana University - Purdue University Indianapolis (IUPUI). **MODERATORS:** Virginia Caine, Director, Marion County Health Department; Janie Canty-Mitchell, Assistant Professor, Indiana University School of Nursing; Barbara Gunn, Executive Director, Glick Foundation; Dennis Jones, CEO, Midtown Community Mental Health Center, Doris Merritt, Associate Dean, Indiana University School of Medicine; Robert Moore, Vice President, Indiana Hospital and Health Association; Michael Rodman, Vice President, NBD Bank.

Introduction

The relationship between philanthropy and health care is complicated and longstanding, and destined to gain even more significance in light of changing health care delivery systems and funding sources. This trend particularly applies to nurses, who represent the largest of the health care professions and the professionals most likely to play boundary-spanning roles in reformulated systems. Nurses in the 21st century will be asked to demonstrate the value of their care in many arenas beyond traditional hospital structures and will manage ventures integral to concepts in philanthropic studies such as mobilizing community action, working with volunteers, fund raising, etc. An understanding of philanthropy—defined as voluntary service, association, and giving for the public good—will be increasingly important to effective professional nursing. (It is for that very reason that Indiana University now offers the first dual-degree program combining master's degrees in nursing administration and philanthropic studies.)

An enlarged role for volunteers in health care is evident across the landscape. Volunteers deliver meals, reminisce with nursing home residents, staff blood drives and rock premature or sick infants in nurseries. As trustees and advocates, they offer advice for policy development to assist health care institutions in becoming more sensitive to the needs of their constituencies, and they raise funds to support clinical research, acquire state-of-the-science technology and create alternate streams of revenue in highly competitive environments. Nurses have a proud history of mobilizing volunteer action for the public good as evidenced in the leadership roles played by Clara Barton (Red Cross), Margaret Sanger (Planned Parenthood), Wilma Scott Heide (National Organization for Women) and others in the founding of key volunteer associations.

A major form of voluntary services is the dedicated care of friends and family members in the home setting where volunteers monitor children on mechanical devices, support individuals with Alzheimer's disease or AIDS, or enable loved ones to spend their last days in the comfort of familiar surroundings rather than in the technological maze of an intensive care unit. Indications are that community-centered care will promote and depend on this kind of caregiving, and that nurses will be the caregiver's link to necessary services, support and expertise. These developments emphasize the need for nurses to have a better understanding of working with volunteers. Indeed, understanding such caregiving within the four-sector model (public, for-profit, non-profit and family) may be a way of lending added prestige to such activities.

The interrelationships between nursing and philanthropy go far beyond volunteer management issues, however. In an increasingly competitive environment, nurse leaders are being asked to play a major role in obtaining needed resources, from effective articulation of their institution's mission/vision to cultivation of prospective donors. Previously, nursing education has not paid much attention to these matters, nor has it explicitly addressed the concept of the nurse as philanthropist. Indeed, nurses as a group may be predisposed to shy away from that descriptor, thinking either that they "give at the office" or get paid too little to be donors themselves. However, it is in providing community service and giving to worthy causes that nurses may best connect themselves (and their causes) effectively, in turn, to the life of the larger community in which they are embedded.

Foundations are organizations that exist, typically, to leverage philanthropic dollars into creative programs of a model-developing nature. Nurses are increasingly playing a leadership role in setting such priorities, for example, Rebecca Rimel (The Pew Charitable Trusts) and Susan Sherman (The Independence Foundation). They are also taking the lead in founding major initiatives that come into existence through philanthropic dollars, such as Bernadine Lacey's and Ruth Lubic's work in Washington, DC, developing, respectively, a homeless shelter and a maternity center.

One could argue that both nursing and philanthropy have gained professional respectability in recent years; one could also argue that their shared values are under siege at the present time when rugged individualism shapes so much of American thinking. The papers that follow will explore some of the common concerns of nursing and philanthropy for the purpose of celebrating their shared traditions, articulating what the fields can learn from each other, and pointing to how they might work together in the future. These proceedings begin with a historical overview of the role played by the W. K. Kellogg Foundation in furthering the profession of nursing. Helen K. Grace (actual presenter) and Gloria R. Smith have played major leadership roles in that foundation, and they bring their collective experience to ask provocatively whether nurses can present a united front in setting a reform agenda that foundations can support. Sara Fry's paper builds on that theme; it reviews various examples of nursing service in light of an endangered nursing ethic that might be revitalized by showing how the values of nursing can meet the current challenges of practice.

The next three papers plumb specific topics of concern to nursing and philanthropy. Sharon Farley reflects on volunteer-professional partnerships in light of her rich community health experience. Robyn Gibboney analyzes the burgeoning service-learning movement in relationship to nursing education. Joyce Fitzpatrick uses her extensive experience as dean to explore the philanthropic appeal of nursing. Robert Payton's and Angela McBride's papers are philosophical in nature. As a professor of philanthropy, Payton explores commonalities between philanthropy and professionalism in their regard for the public good; as a professor of nursing, McBride wonders if the shared concept of stewardship might not unite the two fields. Finally, Warren Ilchman's paper urges specific actions; because he is not a nurse and thus cannot be accused of self interest, his valuing of the role that nurses can play in achieving civil society may be particularly empowering.

The themes explored in these proceedings are not meant to be exhaustive but illustrative of the new thinking that might result from taking seriously the link between nursing and philanthropy. To the extent that one can think of nursing as philanthropy or philanthropy as nursing, such metaphorical reflections can serve an energizing effect in making new connections and empowering both fields to exert the leadership inherent in action for the public good. Given current admonitions to break down disciplinary lines in order to see the big picture, nursing and philanthropy might unite to make sure that the public good is in the picture.

1

Nursing's Role in Mobilizing Public Response

Yesterday, Today and Tomorrow

Helen K. Grace • Gloria R. Smith

What does it take to mobilize a public response? Why has nursing had such a difficult time? How could we be more effective? These were the questions that came to mind in beginning to frame this presentation. Mobilizing a public response for something first of all requires that the person or entity be sufficiently visible to be recognized as an entity to be supported. The *User Manual and Thesaurus for the Foundation Directory,* (Foundation Center, 1997) a tool for retrieval of information related to grants, lists only two headings for nursing in a fifty-page thesaurus—Nursing care and Nursing, general. Nursing homes are also referenced, but nursing as an entity, in and of itself, is nearly invisible. Medicine, in contrast has multiple listings, and in fact, nursing is referenced as subsumed under medicine. Even more discouraging is the listing of foundations that include grant making to nurses in their statements related to scope of grant making. The list generated from the categorization of the Foundation Center is extremely limited and devoted primarily to small local foundations who make small grants, primarily scholarships, to students pursuing nursing careers. While this is an incomplete listing of support for nursing in the philanthropic world, given the larger number of grants that are made to causes headed by nurses, yet the reality of the invisibility of nursing as an identifiable entity in its own right is revealing. From this it might be concluded that particularly in the foundation world, nursing is not widely recognized as an entity for the flow of philanthropic dollars. Secondly, if one is to be effective in mobilizing a response, it is important that there be an understanding of the philosophical or value base that underlies the actions of any one of the parties to the exchange. As I've lived and worked in the environment of a foundation for the past fifteen years, I am repeatedly struck by the divergence of the cultures of nursing and philanthropy. Waldemar Nielsen, a prominent scholar of foundations, notes that "Foundations, even the largest, are typically the lengthened shadows of a few individuals, and a study of them has to begin with a study of their creators." He further notes that "without exception, all of the builders of the fortunes on which these huge foundations were based are men ... in few instances women have been prominent essentially as trouble-makers and gadflies." He concludes that "On the whole, however, large-scale philanthropy is made up of male dominated organizations" (Waldemar Nielsen, 1985). Boards and executives have predominantly been white males. While the foundation world is slowly changing, the value sets that guided their early formation prevails to this day in the philanthropic community.

The male-oriented business culture of the philanthropic world operates from a far different philosophical and value framework than that of the female-oriented, nurturing nursing profession. The agenda for support of nursing in both the public and private sector has by and large been set by forces outside of nursing. Had nursing been able to coalesce and form a unified agenda from within the profession, it is likely that nursing could have been much more effective in shaping and capitalizing on the potential of private and public funding.

This paper will analyze this clash of cultures and the difficulties nursing has had in making effective connections, and thereby mobilizing significant responses, expressed in financial support from the philanthropic community. While I will draw heavily upon the Kellogg Foundation and its long-standing relationship with nursing, a more general analysis of support for nursing from the private sector will also be drawn. In using the Kellogg Foundation as a case study for purposes of this study, I am drawing heavily upon the work of Joan Lynaugh in an as yet unpublished manuscript, *Philanthropy and*

American Nursing: the Case of the W. K. Kellogg Foundation, 1930-1980 (Lynaugh, 1994), as well as my current research into the overall programming of the Kellogg Foundation from 1930 to the present.

THE KELLOGG FOUNDATION AND NURSING

The Kellogg Foundation has had the longest sustained relationship to the nursing profession of any source of funding, public or private, and the funding that has gone to nursing consistently exceeds that of all other foundations combined. Since its establishment, nurses have been employed on the staff of the Kellogg Foundation. Established in 1930 with a primary concern for the welfare of children, the early orientation of the Kellogg Foundation was strongly influenced by the White House Conference on Children and Youth convened by the then President Herbert Hoover. Mr. Kellogg, as was common with other philanthropists of his time, called upon his personal connections to help him put his ideas into place. The first part-time director of the Kellogg Foundation was Dr. Andrew Selman, a medical missionary to China who had returned to the United States and was the medical director in the Kellogg Company. He had first gained the attention of Mr. Kellogg for his treatment of him when he fell ill with pneumonia while visiting China. Later, as the foundation grew, another physician, Stuart Pritchard, a Canadian physician employed at the Kellogg Sanitarium and noted public health educator, was appointed as the first full-time president. Thus, early in the life of the Kellogg Foundation, the overarching interest in the welfare of children was joined to the growing public health movement in this country. The first major work of the Kellogg Foundation was to put in place, in a seven-county area of Michigan, a model for the organization of comprehensive health services in rural areas. Nurses were at the heart of this demonstration project. As Lynaugh observes, "Lulu St. Clair (Blaine) the Foundation's first nurse and the MCHP director of health education from 1933 to 1936, organized a corps of public health nurses called the Flying Squadron. These nurses traveled the counties organized under the

MCHP using their preparation in public health and education to teach not only children but their teachers the ways of hygiene, good nutrition, detection of health problems and preventive health services." As many as 29 nurses were employed by the Kellogg Foundation in the thirties—all with advanced preparation as public health nurses, and some with specialization in maternal-child health. These nurses were the backbone of the Michigan Community Health Project making an interface between the child in the school, their families, doctors, dentists and a network of social support services, such as youth clubs, summer camps and remediation services for children with special needs. A highly effective home maternity nursing service was also a part of this original work in which nurses provided prenatal care, went to the homes to be with the mothers in the early stages of labor, called the physicians to do the deliveries, and did most of the postnatal follow-up including well-child care. While much of the work of the nurses in the MCHP was somewhat invisible, and they were working in a framework constructed from a medical perspective, they were amazingly effective in putting together a quality "seamless" comprehensive health care system that worked amazingly well, and was truly a model of nursing practice.

With this comprehensive demonstration project in place, the next focus of attention was on the professional competence of those providing services to children: physicians, dentists, nurses, school teachers and a variety of youth-related workers. Adult continuing education became an area to be supported by foundation funds. Later, the use of the MCHP as a training site for health professionals to learn about public health in rural settings led to what was described as the creation of the "field university." Health professionals from throughout the United States, Canada and later Latin America came for field experience in this seven-county area of Michigan. Nurses were amply represented both in receiving support for participation in a wide array of continuing education offerings, as well as in the extensive fellowship program which was part of the "field university." Nurses, along with other health professionals, came from all over the United States for field experiences in community health. This initiated a long-standing relationship between the Kellogg Foundation and nursing education, particularly the programs developing in universities.

THE WAR YEARS

The work of the Kellogg Foundation changed dramatically with the coming of World War II. The foundation consciously committed its resources to "Winning the War," and the diverting of resources to the war effort. In the health area, extensive consultations had been held with the relevant departments of the government and health professions educators as to what the Kellogg Foundation might contribute to the war effort. A major concern was for production of adequate numbers of health professionals to attend to the sick and the injured as part of the war effort while maintaining the health of the citizenry. The medical schools had addressed the problem by proposing to accelerate their programs by running them year round, provided that there were no mandates to reduce the quality of the educational programs. While this was the "solution" proposed by the educators, medical students relied upon summer employment to finance their medical education. The federal government recognized this as a major problem that might result in fewer students completing medical school rather than the increase they were hoping to stimulate. Securing the necessary legislation to put a scholarship and loan program in place that was publicly funded would require at least a year. The Kellogg Foundation was asked to fill this void by funding such a program. Within four months, the field had been assessed as to the average amount of money a student earned by summer employment, and scholarship funds were placed in every medical school in the U.S. and in Canada along with some loan funds, that were designed to create a lasting funding base for support of students in their medical school studies. A similar approach was taken to dentistry, but when the same model was to be applied to nursing, the question immediately arose as to which of the multitude of nursing educational programs should be supported. While nursing received its fair share of the scholarship and loan funds (fifty-three grants totaling $159,000 were granted to university-linked programs), the model was not an appropriate one for nurses (most did not have to pay for tuition as the training schools were run by hospitals), and they were already on a year-round accelerated model.

As the war developed, Lynaugh notes that two veterans of World War I tried to get nursing to face up to the war emergency. "Julia Stimson, President of the American Nurses Association, sought to avoid the factionalism she believed seriously weakened nursing's response to World War One. Mary Beard, Director of the Red Cross Nursing Service, knew that the traditional source of military nurses, the Red Cross First Reserve, was no solution to the insufficient number of nurses available for military service." By 1940, nursing leaders such as Isabel Stewart were advocating creation of a commission representative of nursing as a whole. Finally, after numerous letters back and forth amongst the nursing leaders of the day, the National Nursing Council (this council was later known as the National Nursing Council on War Service—NNCWS) was created, which brought together the nursing organizations of the day and departments of the federal government involved with nursing. As Lynaugh notes "it is here that the story of the long-standing relationship between the Kellogg Foundation and American nursing really begins. The Foundation's interest in nursing changed from local public health funding to influencing national public health policy" (Lynaugh, in press, pp. 42-43).

ATTEMPTS TO UNIFY NURSING

The National Council on Nursing represented the following organizations: the American Nurses Association, National Organization of Public Health Nurses, National League of Nursing Education, Association of Collegiate Schools of Nursing, National Association of Colored Graduate Nurses and a cross section of national service agencies including the American Red Cross. The task confronting this group was to find 3,000 nurses per month plus recruit students into nursing schools. This was a monumental task given the voluntary nature of the organization. Mary Beard, who had worked with the Rockefeller Foundation approached the Kellogg Foundation in 1942 to fund the work of the organization. Between 1942 and 1945 the Kellogg Foundation contributed $331,500 to keep the council going. Later the recruitment functions of NCNWS were taken over by the federal government and the attention of this council turned to other matters. To the nursing leaders of the day the war was seen as an opportunity to unite nursing. Elmira Bears Wickenden saw a chance to work out nursing's perennial problems: its dysfunctional educational system, the poorly organized systems in which nurses worked, and their low pay (Lynaugh, pg. 41).

In retrospect, instead of uniting nursing, the war consolidated some of the divisions that were already in place. As the National Council for Nursing operated through the years, the foundation repeatedly pushed them toward becoming a unifying force in nursing. At one point the then President of the Kellogg Foundation, Emory Morris, wrote to Mary Sheehan, Chair of the NNCWS Planning Committee "we are delaying any assistance ... until after the final structure of the professional nursing organization of this country has been established." Despite the fact that six more years would go by before restructuring of the ANA and the other participatory organizations occurred, the Kellogg Foundation continued to fund many nursing projects. Two early studies of nursing were spawned by the National Nursing Council on War Services—first the Brown report *Nursing for the Future*, and second, that of the National Commission for the Improvement of Nursing Services, which was to implement the recommendations made by Esther Lucille Brown. Despite these early efforts to unify nursing, a theme that has persisted through the years is that of the Kellogg Foundation trying to nudge the nursing organizations into a unified posture vis-a-vis public and private funding sources, and nursing remaining divided. While support for the work of Esther Lucille Brown came through the NNCWS, later efforts such as the National Commission for the Study of Nursing and Nursing Education ($609,187, 1966), for the National Joint Practice Commission ($667,226, 1977), and for the National Commission on Nursing Implementation (NCNIP) ($2,351,245, 1984; $27,375, 1989) were concerted efforts supported by the Kellogg Foundation to bring unity to the nursing profession. While these commissions have worked diligently, and have made repeated recommendations, once the external funding has ceased, the divisiveness continues.

Why has this been such an important issue from the perspective of the Kellogg Foundation, and why has its importance been ignored, despite these massive efforts and large infusion of funding? From the perspective of the Kellogg Foundation, the answer to this question is readily apparent in reviewing the context of other ongoing programming. Nursing has simply not been able to set its priorities within the profession in such a way that public and private funders can make the links. Any area that the Kellogg Foundation might "touch" could inadvertently lead them into a position of taking "sides" on some of the internal conflicts within nursing. Reviewing unpublished reports to the board of the various advisory groups in the health field from 1945 to 1965 is revelatory. For example, as the war was drawing to a conclusion, the advisory committee on medicine, composed of highly visible leaders in the field, set their priorities upon the improvement of graduate medical education, based on the need to re-tool and re-certify physicians whose careers had been disrupted by the war. There was no ambiguity about the priorities of medicine and they spoke with one voice. In contrast, the Nursing Advisory Committee was all over the map—concerned with meeting the demands for persons to staff the burgeoning hospital system, coupled with an interest in moving nursing education into the educational mainstream. What were the funding priorities? Without a clear statement from nursing as to its priorities, the agenda for nursing was shaped largely from outside the profession. The need of hospitals for adequate numbers of staff pushed the agenda for licensed practical nurses. Without a clear consensus as to the directions that nursing was setting for itself, the funding of the Kellogg Foundation was particularly vulnerable to the pressures exerted from other areas within the foundation. Following World War II, Lynaugh notes, "The post War emphasis on hospital development and expansion as the center piece of the health system accentuated the pre-existing concern and debate about the supply and quality of nurses. The Kellogg staff's simultaneous goals of moving nurse preparation into the educational mainstream and expanding hospitals placed them squarely in the middle of the complex and long-running argument about nursing's role in the health care system" (p. 71). The funding of the Kellogg Foundation in the post-World War II period is reflective of these concerns. Between 1944 and 1952, the Kellogg Foundation invested nearly a million dollars on graduate-post-graduate nursing education. At the same time, $895,402 was directed toward testing the liensed vocational nurses concept. The studies of Mildred Montag leading to the development of two-year associate degree programs in nursing contributed another dimension as to how sufficient nurses could be produced to staff hospitals. The infusion of this work force into hospital settings, and the need for management of this work force, led to an emphasis upon nursing service administration. Nowhere is the conflict between the concerns for the *quantity* of nurses versus concerns for the *quality* of their preparation more apparent than in the deliberations of the Nursing Advisory Committee in their attempts to be responsive to the demands placed upon the profession. As a result, the funding of the Kellogg Foundation in its attempts to be responsive to the recommendations of nursing leadership poured money into the development of practical nurse education, funded movement of liberal arts colleges into offering baccalaureate nursing programs, supported development of associate degree nursing programs and development of graduate programs for nurses, all simultaneously.

Changes in the Playing Field

In 1965, a major change occurred in the organization of programming at the Kellogg Foundation. From 1945 to 1965, advisory committees had been overseers of the work of the divisions—Medicine, Public Health, Nursing, Dentistry. For twenty years these committees working with a staff department head employed by the Kellogg Foundation reviewed the programming in a particular area, assessed the needs within the field and made recommendations, even to the level of the grants that should be made. As the foundation increased its assets, and the scope of its grant making extended world wide, the new president of the foundation, Russell Mawby, was concerned that there was little or no communication amongst the various divisions. The advisory committees were disbanded, and the departments dissolved. Areas of interest such as agriculture and adult continuing education developed, and health programming became integrated across the health disciplines.

From this point forward, nursing was placed at a peer level within the health programming area of the foundation and needed to compete as an equal with the other health professions. The nursing program director—Barbara Lee from 1967-1981, Helen Grace from 1982-1995 and Gloria Smith, 1995 to the present—has been part of the programmatic decision-making structure, and has been a spokesperson for nursing. As such, the challenge has been to participate in the shaping of integrated goals to guide the grant making process and then working to bring grants forward that are related to the programming priorities that have been established by the board of trustees. Bear in mind the context of foundations that has previously been described as operating from a business perspective and from a male-dominated cultural point of view. The internal work of nurses within the foundation has been that of participating in creating a "playing field" in which nurses are important players. The other side of the equation then, is for nursing and nurses to figure out "how to play the game" and to initiate ideas for grants that would "fit" within the broad framework of programming priorities. The health goals that have governed internal decision-making at the Kellogg Foundation since 1965 include the following: "Assuring Quality Health Care and Health Professions Education", "Improving Access to and Availability of Health Care," "Providing for Cost Containment and Increased Productivity of Health Care," "Community Wide, Coordinated, Cost Effective Health Services," "Betterment of Health," "Advancing Health Promotion, Disease Prevention and Public Health," "Community-Based Health Services," and most recently, "Integrated, Comprehensive Health Systems." In reviewing these titles, it is readily apparent that the "playing field" has been in place in the health field that is supportive of nurses as key players, and of nursing defining its place within a multidisciplinary context.

In addition to the areas of support that are specific for health, nursing has benefited from support for work related to adult continuing education and leadership. An analysis of grants made from 1930 to 1990 shows that funding for projects in the United States in which nurse or nursing appears in the purpose statement totaled $89,056,314. An additional $22,000,000 was directed toward nursing internationally, primarily to Latin America and the Caribbean, Africa, Australia and Canada. This total does not include projects in which nursing has played a major leadership role but the specific word nurse does not appear in the purpose statement, nurses who have been participants in the national and international fellowship programs of the Kellogg Foundation, or major multidisciplinary initiatives, such as the Community Partnerships: Health Professions Education, or Community Based Public Health in which the design of the program mandated full participation of nursing. Given these parameters, and the grant making that has occurred from 1990 to the present, a conservative estimate of the dollars that have flowed to nursing from the Kellogg Foundation would be in the vicinity of $200 million, not a small amount, given the limited nature of private philanthropic dollars to move nursing forward as a full participant in this context.

During the time span from 1965 to the present, the "playing field" has shifted several times. In the sixties and seventies, the major playing field was in the hospital setting. The Kellogg Foundation was a major supporter of the development of the health service administration field. As the emphasis in health care increasingly turned to hospitals as the focal point of the health care system, not surprisingly a major area of concern for the Kellogg Foundation became that of supporting nursing service administration programs to improve the management of hospitals. This was followed by a concern for the quality of clinical practice in hospital settings. While the earlier emphasis had been upon education of practitioners in a variety of educational programs, in the late sixties, the concern was for quality practice. Remaining consistent in its support for the health professionals to work together, funding for a wide range of joint practice projects, and for the National Joint Practice Commission are reflective of this concern. Other efforts to improve the practice of nurses were in the long-term care area and in the preparation of geriatric nurse practitioners.

In the mid-eighties, the playing field shifted to the community. In re-examining its programming priorities, a concern emerged that the agenda for foundation funding was being driven primarily by hospitals and by health professions, particularly medicine. A very deliberative change in programming priorities occurred shifting the focus from hospital-based care to community-based health services. As the programming priorities shifted, the work that nurses were doing at the community level quickly gained the attention of the health program staff at the Kellogg Foundation. Nurses working with the elderly, such as in the block nursing programs or in rural settings in Alabama, nurses working with mothers in inner-city Detroit and rural Georgia, and with mothers and children in Battle Creek stepped to the fore in becoming grantees leading an array of innovative projects funded by the Kellogg Foundation. Nurses, and the special relationships that they had built with families and communities, were natural leaders for the project funding of the Kellogg Foundation. With a particular concern for traditionally underserved groups, African Americans, Hispanics and Native Americans, the reach of Kellogg Foundation funding into remote rural areas and into inner cities brought the funding priorities of the Kellogg Foundation in line with the heroic work that nurses were doing that was largely invisible.

But in order for this work to be sustained, and to have an impact on the societal institutions that had responsibility for these underserved populations, the efforts needed to be linked to institutional bases that assured their long-range sustainability. While the spotlight had been successfully shifted to the community and to the health care needs as people perceived them, the next logical step is the linkages of these programs into permanent funding sources. Parish nursing, in which nurses working with community residents find a base of support in integrating their practice into church settings and school-based clinics, is an example of a new funding priority related to comprehensive integrated health care systems. Since the mid-eighties, the support for nurse-led work by the Kellogg Foundation has increased dramatically. In addition, the Kellogg Foundation has placed support solidly behind nursing in becoming a full participant with other health providers in community-based care. The Community Partnerships: Health Professions Education ($47.5 million), Community-Based Public Health ($25 million), the current

Graduate Medical/Nursing Education ($15 million) and Turning Point ($17.5 million) efforts are examples of initiatives to engage nursing as a full partner with other health disciplines.

Within the decision-making structure of the Kellogg Foundation, never has the climate been more supportive of the work that nurses do in providing quality health care to people in a wide array of settings. The infusion of women and diversity within the board of trustees, and the increased diversity of staff at the Kellogg Foundation, including the addition of four nurses (a total of six) as full-time program staff and the setting of programming priorities so compatible with those of nursing, have created an unusually productive opportunity structure.

THE INVISIBILITY OF THE SUPPORT FOR NURSING OF THE KELLOGG FOUNDATION

Why then, given this degree of support for nursing, is the work of the Kellogg Foundation nearly invisible in the eyes of the nursing profession? While individual nurses have risen to the challenge and developed a wide array of proposals that have been funded by the Kellogg Foundation, organized nursing, perhaps because of its long-standing divisions, has been ineffectual in development of creative proposals to compete on the "playing field" which has been created. The playing field requires nursing to take its place at the table as a peer with the other health disciplines and engage in dialogue to reshape the future of health care and health professions education in this country.

Nursing could take the lead in organizing these dialogues. While through the years the nurse leaders within the Kellogg Foundation have had repeated discussions with leaders of professional nursing organizations, nothing seems to occur. Multiple discussions with each of the leading nursing organizations regarding potential approaches to positioning nursing on this broader playing field have led nowhere. Nursing, with support from the Kellogg Foundation, could be taking the lead in bringing the health professions around the table to address health care for underserved populations in this country. Nursing knows more about how this can be done than any of the other disciplines combined. Where is the leadership in nursing that can see beyond their parochial interests of the profession to the larger picture of nursing's critical role in providing quality health care to the American people?

Nursing and Other Funding Sources: Public and Private

While the experiences of the Kellogg Foundation with nursing and vice versa are one part of the story, it is important to look at a broader context to address the overall question of this presentation. Where has nursing been able to "connect" in both the public and private sectors?

In the public sector, the most visible sources of support for nursing are through divisions or institutes specifically created for nursing. The competition for public dollars is for support of these nursing entities, and once the money is allocated, the priority setting is largely within the profession itself. On this playing field, nursing can coalesce its agenda primarily around the allocation of resources to things specifically labeled as nursing. Once this allocation has occurred and the funding guidelines and priorities developed, nursing competes within the profession for the awarding of these dollars. The rules of the game are spelled out, and the competition is within the nursing field, not with other disciplines or professions. And while the relative amount of support for nursing is limited in comparison to that going to other professions, nursing has developed comfort in working on this familiar playing field.

What about the private sector and the relationship of nurses to other foundations? Early support for nursing was primarily for the work that nurses did with the impoverished people of their time. In contrast to the large investment that the Rockefeller Foundation, for example, made in medical education, the amount directed toward nursing education was extremely limited. In reviewing this history, the extensive funding for medical education grew out of a clear agenda for the reforms that were needed. The Rockefeller Foundation was responding to an agenda that had been set from an extensive study and recommendations growing out of that study. In contrast, requests for support of nursing education were fragmented and did not have the power of a clear mandate behind them.

Support for nursing amongst the major foundations has been extremely limited historically, although in recent years more attention has been paid to the important role of nurses within the health care field. The formation of the Robert Wood Johnson Foundation, with its mission "to improve the health and health care of all Americans," opened up a large reservoir of private funding in the health field. How well has nursing done in gaining its fair share of these resources? According to its 1996 annual report, the Robert Wood Johnson Foundation made 875 grants and 71 contracts totaling $266.92 million. Only 23 grants of the 875 (less than 1%) totaling $3,914,709 can be identified as granted to nursing organizations or to causes involving nurses. This does not account for nurses who head projects, such as those related to chronic care, or nurses who are in fellowship programs, but it is fair to conclude that nursing is not doing well in the era of concern for managed care as the overriding issue. A review of other major foundations such as the Pew Charitable Trusts mirrors this assessment. Why is nursing doing so poorly in garnering public and private support?

In the article "A Place at the Table" (*Reflections*, Third/Fourth Quarters 1997), Sara Abrams reviews the history of nursing's relation to the Rockefeller Foundation. She notes that the early foundations were "aimed at social transformation" through addressing the major problems of their time. The original philanthropists were followed by "a new class of bureaucratic managers who created a process of funding within which priorities could be shifted as intellectual and socioeconomic interest changed. Nursing originally won officers' attention, but ultimately lost group in the philanthropic enterprise" (Sara Abrams, p. 18). "Promoting health among immigrant groups in American ghettos, reconstruction of war-ravaged Europe, and fighting the effects of poverty and disease in the rural South may well have been within the scope of the foundation's early mission. Establishment of academic nursing was less clearly linked to either the early mission or its refinement."

Abrams further notes that by the end of the 1920s support for nursing had virtually disappeared from the Rockefeller Foundation and observes that "corporate philanthropies both shape the future and are shaped by the social and political environment in which they operate. Some of the failures of early Rockefeller projects made the directors hesitant to take social and political risks." And the biggest political risks were considered to be the divisions within nursing itself. "One of nurses' strongest allies in the foundation expressed dismay and confusion about divisions within nursing itself" (p. 19). Interestingly, the Kellogg Foundation picked up support for nursing where the Rockefeller Foundation left off. Most of the early work of the Kellogg Foundation was shaped by participation with the Rockefeller Foundation. As Abrams notes, "Perhaps the astonishing thing is that the Rockefeller Foundation provided an early invitation to the game. The misfortune for the nursing profession was that it was not yet ready to play." The Kellogg Foundation picked up the mantle, and has continued to find ways to maintain significant support for nursing. Continuation of this source of support cannot be maintained by those working within the foundation alone, but must be joined by nurses and nursing outside the foundation walls that can come together in a united front with clearly established priorities and a commitment to working together for the improvement of health and health care in this country. Nursing has not found ways to "get its act together" to date—its future base of support in both the public and private sector is dependent upon how well we can deal with our internal conflicts, and how we take our place at the broader table concerned with comprehensive health care for all. This is yet another plea for nursing leaders who can rise above their own parochial interests and play at the larger table. The stakes are very high.

References

Abrams, S. (1997). A Place at the Table, Reflections, 23(3), 18-19.

User Manual and Thesaurus for the Foundation Directory (1997). New York, The Foundation Center.

Lynaugh, J. (unpublished). Philanthropy and American Nursing: The Case of the W. K. Kellogg Foundation, 1930-1980. National League for Nursing.

Nielsen, W. (1985). The Golden Donors: A New Anatomy of the Great Foundation. New York: Truman Talley Books/E. Dutton, pp. 11-14.

2

Doing Good

FROM PATERNALISM TO A NURSING ETHIC

Sara T. Fry

Throughout the world, the fundamental responsibility of the nurse is understood to have four components (ICN, 1973): 1) to promote health, 2) to prevent illness, 3) to restore health, and 4) to alleviate suffering.

This is what nurses do. In carrying out this responsibility, nurses provide a service to individuals, families and communities. They also coordinate this service with the services of other health workers. The key word here is "service." "To serve" means to act in a particular capacity: to provide certain goods or to be of assistance to someone (Morris, 1976). "To serve" also means to meet or satisfy a need. Providing a service is the act or means of serving. So when we say that nurses provide a service, we are actually saying that nurses provide certain "goods" that can be of assistance to people and that satisfy or meet some particular need that they have. The "goods" provided are the diagnostic, therapeutic and ethical judgments of nurses derived from their assessments of patients' physical, emotional and spiritual states. Nurses make judgments about how these states are affecting a patient's health and well-being, and what interventions are needed to improve health and well-being.

The specific service provided by nurses is *nursing care* and the need for this service is universal (Leininger, 1984). All people, at some time or another, need nursing care. In its most simplistic terms, nursing care is "assisting an individual, sick or well, in the performance of those activities contributing to health or its recovery (or to peaceful death) that he would perform unaided if he had the necessary strength, will or knowledge" (Henderson, 1977, rev. ed.). This is the service that nurses provide.

In this presentation, I am going to briefly highlight some of the forms that this tradition of service has taken throughout nursing's history. I will argue that service is the single most important and central theme throughout nursing's history. And it is this theme that links nursing to philanthropy in significant ways. Second, I will briefly trace the development of nursing's ethic to the present time. Third, I will describe the fundamental moral concepts and moral values of nursing that underlie the tradition of service and that form the nursing ethic. Since nursing care is always directed toward individuals, families and/or communities within a need relationship, I will argue that the relationships formed by nursing care are necessarily covenantal. Last, I will argue that "doing good" as a nurse, in these last few years of the twentieth century, is an endangered ethic and suggest ways that nursing and philanthropy can complement each other in preserving the existence of nursing's service to the public.

THE TRADITION OF SERVICE

Throughout history, nursing has been associated with a particular kind of service to others. The Roman matrons—Marcella, Fabiola and Paula—were women known for their charitable works, spirituality, intelligence and wealth. They devoted themselves to the care of the sick poor and established places for the sick poor to receive nursing care (Donahue, 1985). Fabiola established the first free Christian hospital in her own palace. Paula built hospices for pilgrims and hospitals for the sick along the road to Bethlehem. Paula is credited with the first systematic training program for nurses and the teaching of nursing as an art, as well as a service. In describing the work of these early nurses, St. Jerome said, "they trim lamps, light fires, sweep floors, clean vegetables, put heads of cabbage in the pot to boil, lay table cloths, and set tables, hand cups, help to wash dishes, and run to and from to wait on others" (as cited in Donahue, 1985, p. 115). In truth, there is not much here to designate these services as "nursing services," as we now know them!

It was not until the Christian church took responsibility for the care of the sick that nursing care began to be recognized. One of the more well-known hospitals established by the church was the Santo Spirito Hospital in Rome, established in 717 AD by order of the Pope (Donahue, 1985). The care in these hospitals, however, was not usually respected or valued. The nursing care was not well organized and hospitals were known to be places of infection and death. As the incidence of disease increased, the numbers of those willing to work as nurses decreased. There would often be more than one patient to a sickbed and patients were ill fed and dirty. Persons of low character were recruited to work as nurses and the quality of nursing care was very low and remained so for a long period of time (Donahue, 1985).

Beginning in the late 1700s and into the 1800s, social and humanitarian reforms took place that had a positive effect on hospitals and the care of the sick throughout the world. Elizabeth G. Fry, a philanthropist and a Quaker, is remembered for her prison work and for founding a society for visiting nurses in London (Donahue, 1985). Called the Society of Protestant Sisters of Charity, the nurses were prepared for home nursing but received no classroom or theoretical instruction for their activities.

Formal instruction in nursing care came to England after Florence Nightingale visited the Deaconess Institute at Kaiserswerth, Germany. At Kaiserswerth, Nightingale observed that the deaconesses received three years of "training" that included visiting nursing, theoretical and bedside instruction in the care of the sick, religious and ethics instruction, and pharmacology. She later studied in Paris under the Sisters of Charity at the Maison de la Providence, and on her return to London in 1853, assumed the position as superintendent of the Institution for the Care of Sick Gentlewomen in Distressed Circumstances (Woodham-Smith, 1983). Before she could establish formal nursing services, war in the Crimea broke out and Nightingale was provided an unprecedented opportunity—she was asked by Sir Sidney Herbert to assemble a small group of nurses for service at the Barrack Hospital at Scutari.

Faced with the care of 4,000 wounded and sick soldiers at the 1,700-bed Barrack Hospital, Nightingale made the most of her resources—her faith, intelligence and knowledge; a cadre of only 38 nurses; and the support of Sir Sidney Herbert, the secretary of war. The nursing services provided were monumental. In six months' time, the death rate of 42.7% was reduced to 2.2% (Donahue, 1985). She established five diet kitchens, a laundry, canteens for recreation, and demonstrated the use of statistics to document the effects of nursing care on the health of the British soldier. By the time she returned to England, she had changed the image of nursing, and the tradition of nursing service began to evolve to its modern form.

In America, the tradition of service in nursing took several forms. One form was providing nursing relief services during national calamities such as famine, fire, floods or pestilence. The Red Cross Nursing Service, which often acted as a supplement to the regular army and navy nurses as needed, is a good example of this form of nursing service (Donahue, 1985).

A second form was nursing the wounded during wartime. The Spanish-American War, for example, had an acute need for contract nurses to augment regular forces. Many of the soldiers stationed in Cuba contracted yellow fever and contract nurses were helpful to their care. Trying to control the disease, army physicians conducted experiments using human volunteers who were bitten by mosquitos under controlled conditions. The first volunteers were physicians, but nurses were also asked to participate in the experiments. One nurse, Miss Clara Maas, actually gave her life to the cause. Thinking that she would be more useful in Cuba if she developed immunity to yellow fever, she requested that she be bitten by an infected mosquito (Donahue, 1985). The affected mosquitos were applied to her arm but, unfortunately, she developed a hemorrhagic case of yellow fever from which she died within a week.

To honor Clara Maas' rather unique service to humanity, the United States issued a commemorative stamp in 1976 on the 100th anniversary of her birth (Donahue, 1985). This was, by the way, the first U.S. stamp to honor an individual nurse for her service.

A third form that the tradition of service took in the United States was visiting nursing. This form of service focused not only on the care of the sick and the relief of suffering, but also on the promotion of health and the prevention of illness. One of the best examples of this form of service was the Metropolitan Life Insurance Visiting Nursing Service, created in 1909 by the efforts of social reformers in collaboration with the insurance industry (Hamilton, 1988). Under criticism by the public for being materialistic, Metropolitan created a Welfare Division to address the needs of the poorer classes. It appointed the then Director of the NY United Hebrew Charities, Mr. Lee Frankel, to manage the division. Frankel soon developed a program of education and support for the prevention of tuberculosis. He planned to hire social workers to implement the program and discussed the plan with a fellow social reformer, Lillian Wald, Director of the Henry Street Settlement House. Miss Wald convinced him that trained nurses could achieve his aims and more. As Wald saw it, nurses could provide health teaching, hands-on-care of the sick and accurate reporting of illness, which would be very useful to Metropolitan (Hamilton, 1988). She convinced Frankel that visiting nurses' services could even lower mortality rates thus increasing the company's profits and image. An agreement was reached, and the MLI Visiting Nursing Service was born.

By the end of the year, the service had spread from New York City to Baltimore, Boston, Chicago, Cleveland, St. Louis and other cities. Using the services of local visiting nurse services, 28,000 policy holders were visited and given nursing care. Within another year, the nursing service was extended to 213 cities in the U.S. and Canada with Metropolitan creating its own visiting nursing service in those cities where no other service existed.

The MLI Visiting Nursing Service was a highly successful service but soon succumbed to a number of social and economic forces. The number of nursing visits declined as the costs of the visits increased. As Hamilton (1988) points out:

> By 1940 the cost of a nursing visit had risen to $3.00, closing the gap between cost of home and hospital care. Metropolitan accountants warned executives that with industrial insurance sales declining, the cost of a nursing visit was becoming prohibitive for the company. ... Although accountants informed Metropolitan nurses of the possible financial crisis, nurses continued to believe that their role did not include grappling with rising costs (pp. 238-239).

After 43 years of service, the Metropolitan Nursing Service closed in 1953. The circumstances of its creation are lessons for partnerships between philanthropy and nursing. The reasons for its demise can, perhaps, help us to understand how the ethic of nursing is presently endangered and how the tradition of service needs to be reinterpreted for the 21st century. But first, what is the "ethic of nursing" and how did it develop?

The Ethic of Nursing

There are many views about the nursing ethic and some have argued that the nursing ethic is a role-specific and "defined" ethic, based on an ethic of medicine and its tradition of paternalism (Veatch, 1981). In my opinion, the nursing ethic is still evolving; therefore, we should let the ethic speak for itself and not try to cast it into one form or another, at the present time. I'm still letting it speak to me so I don't claim to have the final word on the topic. But I do have a few thoughts on how it has been formed and its central values.

Early interpretations of the nursing ethic tend to be associated with the image of the nurse as a chaste, good woman in Christian service to others; also, as an obedient, dutiful servant (Fry, 1995). The nursing ethic was practicing forms of etiquette and keeping one's duty. Nursing etiquette included forms of polite behavior such as neatness, punctuality, courtesy and quiet attendance to the physician. The nurse demonstrated her acceptance of moral duties of nursing by following the rules of etiquette and by being loyal and obedient to the physician (Robb, 1921). Textbooks in nursing described nursing ethics as the ideals, customs and habits associated with the general characteristics of a nurse (Aikens, 1916), and as doing one's duty with skill and moral perfection (Gladwin, 1930). The rules of etiquette were followed in order to promote professional harmony in patient care.

Following World War II, however, the nurse's role in patient care changed. Keeping the rules of etiquette became less important than meeting standards for nurses' moral behavior and following the science of ethics. The nurse was expected to do good for the patient and was beginning to define "doing good." The nurse's moral responsibility was to contribute to patient good with skill and moral perfection. Being competent, having compassion, protecting the patient's dignity, and doing for others were the central elements of what was beginning to be understood as the nursing ethic. This was an obligation model of the nursing ethic and was based on duties of the nurse as expressed in the nursing code of ethics.

It was not until the patients' rights movement during the 1950s that the nursing ethic evolved to an ethic based on the service nature of the nurse-patient relationship. The image of the nurse as the physician's obedient helper carrying out her duties was replaced by an image of the nurse as an independent practitioner who could be held accountable for what had been done or not done in providing nursing care. Rather than someone who carried out the decisions made by others, the nurse now claimed authority and moral responsibility for specific clinical judgments in patient care. "Doing good" for the patient, where the nurse was concerned, was thus redefined in terms of the moral concepts and values of nursing.

MORAL CONCEPTS AND VALUES OF NURSING

Clarity about these concepts and values is very important because they comprise the foundation for nurses' ethical judgments, define the dimensions of the nurse-patient relationship, and are found in the codes of ethics of nursing associations throughout the world (Fry, 1994). They are the concepts of advocacy, accountability, co-operation and caring.

Advocacy. Advocacy is the active support of an important cause (Fry, 1994). The important cause may be the patient's basic human rights, such as his privacy, dignity, informed choice and even his life. The nurse informs the patient of his rights, makes sure that the patient understands these rights, reports infringements of the patient's rights, and may even intervene to prevent violations of the patient's rights. As an advocate, the nurse helps the patient to understand the advantages and disadvantages of various health options in order to make decisions most consistent with his beliefs and values. When the patient is incapable of making choices, the nurse speaks up for the patient's welfare as defined by the patient before he became ill or as now defined by a substitute decision maker.

Accountability. The concept of accountability has two attributes: *answerability* and *responsibility* (Fry, 1994). Accountability is being answerable for how one has carried out his or her responsibilities. To be accountable, the nurse explains how he or she has promoted health, prevented illness, restored health or alleviated suffering, justifying judgments and actions by accepted moral standards or norms. Accountability for what has been done (or not done) in the nursing role is expected in all relationships that the nurse has with patients, employers, other professional care givers and society at large.

Cooperation. Cooperation is an altruistic concept with three attributes: *active participation* with others to provide quality care for patients, *collaboration* in designing approaches to patient care, and *reciprocity* with co-workers (Fry, 1994). In part, cooperation means to consider the values and goals of those who are like-minded as one's own values and goals.

Cooperation fosters networks of mutual support and close working relationships. It is a richer concept than loyalty because it is a condition for people working together toward a mutual goal. In cooperating with another, the nurse sets aside individual goals and interests in order to improve the quality of the patient's life or to do good for the patient.

Caring. Caring is defined as a form of involvement with others that creates concern about how they experience their world (Benner & Wrubel, 1989). It seems to have at least two attributes: it is a way that humans relate to their world and to each other; and it is a response to the human need to be protected and nurtured. In nursing, caring is an attitude of being there for the patient, feeling with and for the patient, and being close to the patient. Caring also involves specific behaviors toward those in need of care. In this sense, caring is often an obligation or duty of the nurse because of the special relationship between patient and nurse that is formed by the need for nursing care.

Consensus on the Concepts

There is growing evidence that these four concepts form a moral foundation for nursing's tradition of service and its ethic. Several years ago, I had the opportunity to study the codes of ethics of most nursing organizations throughout the world. To my surprise, the four concepts were consistently mentioned and given special emphasis.

Advocacy, for example, is often linked with the virtues of courage and heroism in codes of ethics. Some codes of ethics assert that the principles of fidelity and respect for persons are rooted in the advocacy concept. Accountability for the well being of individuals is a central moral concept in the codes of ethics of nursing organizations in well developed countries. It is also present, although less prominent, in the ethical codes of third world countries.

Cooperation is supported in all ethical codes for nurses and is considered essential to patient well being. Since the nurse is often the person who coordinates the activities of the health care team, cooperation with others has moral implications for patient well being. Caring has always been viewed as essential to nursing care and may be the central moral concept of nursing (Fry, 1990; Gadow, 1987). While some consider caring a moral virtue for nursing (Knowlden, 1990), others consider caring a "moral art" (Benner & Wrubel, 1989), and the science of nursing (Nortveldt, 1996).

Covenantal Model of the Nursing Care Relationship

Because there is consensus among nurses throughout the world that these four concepts provide a moral foundation for the work of nursing and shape the nursing ethic, there is remarkable agreement, as well, on the moral values of nursing. These values are honesty (or truthfulness), compassion, respect for others, doing good for others, competence and keeping commitments.

These values indicate that the nursing care relationship is truly a covenantal one and not just a relationship of obligations or duty (Raines, 1997). I use the term "convenant" to mean that the nursing care relationship has certain elements that make it more than a contracted relationship within which code behaviors or certain services are obliged to take place (May, 1975; Stenberg, 1979). First, the relationship is responsive to individual needs and is directed toward the welfare of the patient. Second, the services provided extend beyond nursing self-interests and anticipate that the patient is a reciprocal party in the nurse-patient relationship. Third, the relationship is based on a commitment to be faithful; thus, is nourished by nursing care rather than limited by it.

This is what nurses offer to patients and to the public—a covenantal relationship responsive to patients' needs. It includes a promise to be faithful in providing nursing services to those who need them. Essentially, this is the nursing ethic—a promise to serve or provide nursing care, and fidelity to the promise (May, 1975)

PRESENT CHALLENGES TO THE NURSING ETHIC

Unfortunately, the nursing ethic is an endangered ethic for several reasons. First, nurses are currently doing more good with less resources than ever before. As a 1996 study (Schindul-Rothschild, Berry, & Long-Middleton, 1996) of over 7,000 nurses found, part-time or temporary RNs and unlicensed personnel are being substituted for full-time RNs throughout the United States. They are taking care of more patients, are being cross-trained to take on more nursing responsibilities, and have substantially less time to provide all aspects of nursing care. Major reasons for these changes are cutbacks and alterations in how health care is delivered. In Massachusetts—a state hit very hard by recent cutbacks in RNs—the number of nurses stating that they were going to leave the profession had increased fivefold in less than two years (Schindul-Rothschild, Berry, & Long-Middleton, 1996). Many nurses in the study wrote that they were going to leave nursing because they could not provide patients with adequate nursing care in the current health care environment. What does this say about the service of nursing care and how nurses understand their commitment to doing good?

A second reason that the nursing ethic is endangered is that nurses are now expected to do limited good, or do good within prescribed limits. For example, the case manager for an HMO may tell the nurse visiting a patient recently discharged to their home that the patient is allowed "x" visits from the nurse. The nurse must squeeze whatever good can be done for the patient within the limits set by the HMO. If the nurse makes a clinical judgment that the patient requires more nursing care and follow-up than can be accomplished in the "x" visits allowed, the nurse has to negotiate with the case manager to obtain more home visits. In about half of the situations, extra nursing care visits are not permitted and the nurse leaves the patient's home feeling that he or she did not, in fact, "do good" where good is interpreted as quality care or what the patient actually needs in order to remain healthy and not be at risk for more health care problems. As Mohr & Mahon (1996) point out, these types of problems are "dirty hands" situations in that the nurse has been required to take part in or implement an immoral project.

A third reason for an endangered ethic is profit-driven incentives that can compromise clinical judgments about patient care needs. Such incentives make it difficult for nurses to exercise their judgments about patients' nursing care needs. Nurses in all settings and specialties are reporting that they are expected to tailor their judgments to the guidelines set by their employers and may find themselves unable to adhere to professional ethical guidelines. They either forgo their nursing values and become part of the profit-driven enterprise or continually compromise their ethical standards in order to stay employed (Mohr, 1996).

A fourth reason is that nurses are taking on more responsibilities in the health care environment than direct patient care. They may be supervising a variety of health care workers, doing budgets, arranging in-service education for these workers and so forth. While they are doing these activities, non-nurses are providing patient care. RNs are still responsible for this care, but their attention to this care is shared with an attention to non-patient care activities. As a result, nurses are finding it harder and harder to honor the nursing ethic—the promise to be faithful and fidelity to the promise.

Finally, many nurses report that they need other skills in order to be an ethical nurse. Knowing the professional code of ethics, using good clinical judgment, and understanding how to apply ethical principles to patient care situations are no longer sufficient skills for one to be an ethical nurse. Nurses need to have superior communication skills in order to raise ethical questions about a patient's care with physicians and other staff who often do not value the nurse's information about the patient. They need assertiveness training in order to defend patients' rights within an increasingly non-rights-responsive health care system. They need to have good negotiation skills in order to work with for-profit, managed-care case managers. They need skills of persuasion in order to bring different members of the health care team to consensus about what to do for the patient. They need to know how to use the techniques of ethical compromise so that members of the health care team can agree on a plan of care for the patient and not feel that they have lost their integrity in doing so.

These are all reasons why the nursing ethic is presently endangered. The climate for the delivery of health care in these last few years of the 20th century has changed in much the same way that the climate changed in the 1950s—the cost of health care has dramatically increased while the pattern of health care delivery has changed. Just as changes earlier in this century helped bring about the demise of the Metropolitan Visiting Nursing Service, the present changes have the potential to change the future of nursing care and how it is provided.

I find it very interesting that one of the American Nurses Association's responses to these changes and the challenges to the nursing ethic is a call for a revision of the *Code for Nurses* (1985), our professional code of ethics. During these difficult times, the nursing ethic should be reviewed and, if found wanting, be strengthened and made more explicit for nurses, patients and the public. However, this is not the time to reduce the requirements of the ethical code or to clothe the nursing ethic in meaningless jargon or empty phrases. There is a rich ethical tradition for nursing practice and all nurses need to work together to support this tradition. Our efforts should be directed toward reinterpreting how the moral concepts and values of nursing can meet the present challenges to nursing practice rather than changing the nursing code of ethics for the sake of change. And this is where philanthropy can play a significant role in working with the nursing profession during these challenging times.

Nursing and Philanthropy

Nursing and philanthropy share some common values. Both fields are concerned about the welfare of others and have a commitment to the improvement of the quality of human life (Bremner, 1988). Both fields value reciprocity—as part of the concept of cooperation for nursing and as a principle of "good returning good" in philanthropy (Jeavons, 1991; Martin, 1994). The notion of fairness is also valued by both fields in terms of how health care resources should be distributed by nurses and a focus on solving social problems by philanthropy (Martin, 1994). Maintenance of dignity and integrity is not only valued by both fields but is often the goal of both nursing and philanthropic actions. And last, both fields respect the voluntary nature of personal action—honoring patients' self-determined choices by nursing and encouraging acts of giving by philanthropy (Martin, 1994).

Working from these shared values, there is great promise for collaboration between nursing and philanthropy. Collaborative actions would nourish the ethic of each field and fulfill this conference's goal of mutual efforts between the two fields. The tradition of service in both fields encourages us to consider how nursing and philanthropy have worked together, in the past, and the models of collaboration that will enable us to continue to do so into the next century. To the extent that collaboration can exist between the two fields, there is considerable promise that mutual efforts can have a significant and positive effect on the lives of the members of society.

References

Aikens, C.S. (1916). **Studies in ethics for nurses.** Philadelphia, W.B. Saunders.

American Nurses Association (1985). **Code for nurses with interpretive statements.** Washington, D.C., The Association.

Benner, P. & Wrubel, J. (1989). **The primacy of caring: Stress and coping in health and illness.** Menlo Park, California, Addison-Wesley.

Bremner, R. H. (1988). **American philanthropy,** 2nd Ed,. Chicago, University of Chicago Press.

Donahue, M.P. (1985). **Nursing: The finest art.** St. Louis, C. V. Mosby Company.

Fry, S. T. (1995). Nursing ethics. In Reich, W.T. (Ed.), **Encyclopedia of bioethics,** (rev. ed.), vol. 2, (pp. 1822-1827). New York, Simon and Schuster Macmillan.

Fry, S. T. (1994). **Ethics in nursing practice: A guide to ethical decision making.** Geneva, International Council of Nurses.

Gadow, S. (1980). Existential advocacy: Philosophical foundations of nursing. In Spicker, S.F. and Gadow, S. (Eds.), **Nursing: Images and ideals,** (pp. 79-101). New York, Springer Publishing.

Gladwin, M.E. (1930). **Ethics: Talks to nurses.** Philadelphia, W.B. Saunders

Hamilton, D.B. (1988). Clinical excellence, but too high a cost: The Metropolitan Life Insurance Company Visiting Nurse Service (1909-1953). **Public Health Nursing, 5(4),** 235-240.

Henderson, V. (1977, rev. ed.). Basic principles of nursing care. Geneva, International Council of Nurses. International Council of Nurses (1973). **Code for nurses: Ethical concepts applied to nursing.** Geneva, ICN.

Jeavons, T. (1991). **Learning for the common good.** Washington, D.C., Association of American Colleges.

Knowlden, V. (1990). The virtue of caring in nursing. In Leininger, M. M. (Ed.), **Ethical and moral dimensions of care,** (pp. 89-94). Detroit, Wayne State University Press.

Martin, M.W. (1994). **Virtuous giving: Philanthropy, voluntary service, and caring.** Bloomington, Indiana University Press.

May, W. (1975). Code, covenant, contract or philanthropy. **Hastings Center Report, 5,** 29-38.

Mohr, W. K. (1996). Ethics, nursing, and health care in the age of "reform." **N&HC: Perspectives on Community, 17(1),** 16-21.

Mohr, W. K. & Mahon, M. M. (1996). Dirty hands: The underside of marketplace health care. **Advances in Nursing Science, 19(1),** 28-37.

Morris, W. (Ed.) (1976). **The American heritage dictionary of the English language.** Boston, Houghton Mifflin Company.

Nortveldt, P. (1996). **Sensitive judgment: Nursing, philosophy, and an ethics of care.** Tano Aschehougs Fonteneserie, Norway.

Robb, I.H. (1921). **Nursing ethics: For hospital and private use.** Cleveland, E.C. Koeckert.

Raines, D. A. (August, 1997). **From covenant to contract: How managed care is changing provider/patient relationships.** AWHONN Lifelines, 41-45.

Shindul-Rothschild, J., Berry, D., & Long-Middleton, E. (1996). Where have all the nurses gone? Final results of our patient care survey. **American Journal of Nursing, 96(11),** 25-44.

Stenberg, M. J. (1979). The search for a conceptual framework as a philosophical basis for nursing ethics: An examination of code, contract, context, and covenant. **Military Medicine, 144(1),** 9-22.

Veatch, R. M. (1981). Nursing ethics, physician ethics, and medical ethics. **Law, Medicine, and Health Care, 9(5),** 17-19.

Woodham-Smith, C. (1983). **Florence Nightingale, 1820-1910.** New York, Atheneum.

3

━━━▶◆◀━━━

Volunteer-Professional Partnerships

Sharon Farley

In the climate of budget reductions, professionals and public agencies have an increased interest in using volunteers to maintain service levels (Brudney, 1990; Wasserbauer et al., 1996). Volunteers are often embraced as a cheap source of labor who extend the productivity of paid staff. Volunteers can increase service levels, but programs that retain volunteers do not "use" them, but include them as partners and decision makers.

Today I will share with you a model and philosophical framework for professionals working with volunteers, and some lessons I learned from my volunteer partners. For ten years I worked in partnership with professionals and volunteers in rural Alabama to improve the health and quality of life of community citizens. The projects, which were administered through a school of nursing and partially supported by the W.K. Kellogg Foundation, had the following goals:

• Stimulate rural development involving community volunteer coalitions, leadership training, infrastructure improvement, job training and public education.

• Foster health care systems that include family-centered, community-based service and collaboration among multiple sectors.

• Conduct family assessments and respond to needs with linkage to services, education and appropriate volunteer coalitions.

• Establish school-based community health and resource centers.

I could do a better job of telling this story if some of my partners were here to participate. Partners such as Mrs. Johnson, who baked the best lemon pie I ever tasted and who could also rally and organize volunteers in her small community to tutor forty children after school. And Mr. Townsend, a seventy-eight-year-old retired vocational teacher, who repaired homes of the elderly because he said, "he wanted to help those old people." And Sarah, an unemployed, single mother, who, after completing a home health aide class and finding a job, helped recruit, organize and supervise one hundred volunteers to provide services for the home-bound elderly.

Philosophical Framework

Citizens have an abundant capacity to care about their communities. When professionals work with volunteers in partnerships where decision-making is shared, changes will occur that improve health and quality of life (Farley, 1997). Volunteers as citizens are part of the solution to their community's problems, and it is important to recognize and respect the skills and strengths they offer. This approach of partnering with volunteers builds on the community's capacity and assets (Kretzmann & McKnight, 1993). Volunteers are involved in all activities, including developing goals and action plans, and evaluation. The specific solutions to specific problems are decided with the citizens without the professionals imposing their ideas on the community.

Respecting the dignity and assets of individuals means providing opportunities for all to participate. Since the project was in a rural area where people were known, it was easy to be inclusive. To emphasize this policy of inclusion, staff constantly repeated key ideas such as "working together, we can do wonderful things" and "involve others, not use others."

A basic tenet of this philosophical framework is to go beyond promises. After one of the first volunteer organizational meetings, a man said he wanted to show me something in his community. He took me to a structure with walls and half of the roof completed.

He said a group promised that they would provide the materials for a community building if volunteers would build it. Citizens were excited about the prospect of having a place to gather for social occasions, education and recreation and many volunteered for the work. However, they had been waiting three years for materials to complete the building. He said, "Please don't get these people's hopes up again if you don't plan to stick with us." We remembered that admonition while we worked with the community.

Volunteer coalitions were a vital component in the success of the community health project in rural Alabama. More than three hundred fifty volunteers, many impoverished themselves, provided services to help citizens in their communities. For example, the helping-hand coalition provided friendly visiting, homemaking, personal care, and respite for the elderly and their families. They also assisted the project nurses with assessment, case finding and referral as well as helping the elderly gain access to the fragmented health care system. Volunteers in this coalition were graduates of the Home Health Aide (HHA) course taught by nurses in the project. Sixty percent of the graduates of the HHA course are now employed by home health agencies and nursing homes. The housing coalition improved the access and safety of older persons' homes by building steps, ramps and porches, and replacing roofs, windows and floors. The high school vocational students improved their carpentry skills by participating in these activities under the supervision of a retired teacher.

In small communities, volunteers assisted school-age children with mathematics, reading and science in after-school and summer programs. They also offered recreational activities for families and implemented programs in the arts and humanities. In four of the communities, the parents received adult basic education and job training and were taught parenting skills. Retired school teachers and older residents used story telling to connect children to their history, culture and values. A coalition named BAMA KIDS, whose members were parents, ministers, public officials and the Sheriff's Department provided mentoring, enrichment activities, recreation and tutoring for children identified as at risk.

In collaboration with a community health agency, the School of Nursing established school-based health and resource centers at a middle school and an elementary school. Volunteer community advisory boards at both schools approved policies and planned and evaluated activities of the centers. A nurse coordinated the centers and worked with volunteers and other health and human service agencies to provide comprehensive family-focused services.

Links between volunteer coalitions and professionals were provided through interagency councils that had representatives from health, social service and education agencies. The councils served four purposes: 1) to plan and implement cooperative programs with the volunteers, 2) to assist with volunteer training and quality assurance, 3) to play an advising role to the volunteers and provide linkages between community initiatives and available services and resources, and 4) to communicate with each other and decrease duplication of services.

Project staff, which consisted of two nurses, two social workers, two secretaries and a project director, provided leadership and educational activities for council members that enabled them to implement a community empowerment model and to assume an advisory role instead of a supervisory role for community partnerships. The staff also helped communities organize volunteer coalitions and foster links between those coalitions and health and human services organizations.

The following case illustrates how volunteers working in partnership with health professionals helped a one hundred two-year-old man remain in his home. A member of the housing coalition who was repairing the man's porch called the project nurse because he was concerned that the elderly man was not eating regularly and his house was very unkempt. The gentleman had no living relatives and his nearest neighbors were a mile away. When the nurse visited the home and did an assessment, she found him to be dehydrated and underweight and to have moderate hypertension. The nurse called his physician to obtain an order for home health services. She also contacted the helping-hand volunteers who provided housekeeping, personal care and friendly visiting. He died at home one year later.

Why People Volunteer

Generally, the volunteers, the majority of whom were African-American, did not view their service as philanthropic. Instead they consider this giving as a general obligation (Hall-Russell and Kasberg, 1997). A volunteer for the elderly said, "I volunteer because I am so indebted because of what the Lord gives me. I just love people. I was raised to help others." Another said, "That is what love is about, helping people without pay." Another said, "As a Christian, it is my job to be in service and to help other people. It gives me pleasure." A minister stated that he volunteered to make life better for children in the community. He said, "I like to see them grow and develop. I didn't have anyone to reach out to me or teach me. This is the best thing I have ever done." The volunteers also had a strong sense of community and the need to cooperate to help themselves. A city councilwoman said, "I work in a community where funds and resources are not available. We have to help ourselves."

In the Alabama project, many who participated identified themselves as natural volunteers. They believed they had special talents or skills which they used to help others. One young woman who was attending the home health aide classes told me she was in the class because she had a natural talent for taking care of people. She had returned to Alabama from Chicago to care for her sick mother. When her aunt and uncle became ill, she cared for them also. She said, "This is not something that everyone can do."

Others volunteered for a cause. Volunteers in the cancer support group were concerned about people who were stricken with cancer because they had survived the disease or a family member or friend had died of cancer. Some had a personal interest in becoming a volunteer. One woman said she was interested in attending the home health aide class and being a helping hand because her goal was to be a nurse. She said she could not attend school when she was young. Some people who participated were unintentional or one-time volunteers. In one instance, a member of the BAMA KIDS organization was searching for money to take children to a play. She saw a local attorney at the grocery store and told him of the need. He gave the money even though he was not a consistent volunteer.

Building Successful Partnerships

Some factors are critical to building successful professional-volunteer partnerships which improve the health and quality of life in communities. First, focus on issues that matter most to people in the community. Communities will always have problems and the problems will never be completely eliminated. Therefore, the goal is to focus the community's energies toward those problems that they are willing to work together to solve (Farley, 1997). Often professionals will plan a service for communities without finding out what the citizens want. They then try to recruit volunteers to meet the need that they have identified. When people do not volunteer, they complain about lack of motivation and apathy. When the Alabama project started, staff wanted to organize volunteers to meet traditional health needs of the elderly, but the citizens wanted to begin with repairing the homes of the elderly. The staff learned a valuable lesson: Listen to the community and never assume what they are willing to work together to achieve. One community minister said, "Your project has ears. The staff listens to the people, responds to their needs and changes direction if they have to."

Developing trust is essential to building partnerships in the community. Communities have seen community-based programs come and go without improving lives and so have little faith in professionals' promises. Trust is established when volunteers are assisted to be successful early in the project. When volunteers in rural Alabama decided they wanted to repair elderly people's homes, staff provided the resources so they could build steps, porches and floors to make the homes safer. One volunteer said, "I didn't think you all could get the boards so fast, but you did. What houses do we work on next Saturday?" Also, to build trust, it is sometimes necessary to deliver something of real value to the community. With the financial assistance provided by the W.K. Kellogg Foundation, a much needed potable water system was build in the rural area. The water was a tangible symbol that the project would provide a benefit to the community. Citizens used this symbol to motivate their neighbors to volunteer.

Building trusting partnerships in communities takes time, patience and persistence. It is necessary to take the long view, and recognize that evolutionary change is a slow process, but more often leads to lasting results. Professionals who support community partnerships must have the patience to overcome problems, barriers and failures. Staff in the Alabama project experienced relatively high levels of stress in the process of building partnerships with volunteers because they had to learn to practice in a new way. The nurses and social workers moved from delivering services to patients and clients to working with citizens as equal, decision-making partners. Also, their work environment changed from bureaucracies that were ordered and managed to the community which was unorganized and unpredictable. They had to learn to tolerate failure. People who live in bad situations are sometimes the least organized and the most angry and despondent (Dewar, 1990).

Developing strong local leaders is essential to sustaining volunteer participation. The goal of the project was to build organizations of volunteers that would continue activities even if the professionals were not present. Continuous formal and informal leadership training was the key to building successful volunteer organizations. Staff learned that one-shot leadership training that consisted of an organized program of meetings, seminars and workshops that lasted one day or one week did not work. Leadership had to be continuous and coincide with the participants' current needs. If the program was not relevant to the volunteers' situation and if they could not apply it, they often forgot what they had learned. Staff helped them practice the skills and reinforced their learning with positive experiences. The staff learned early not to assume who the community leaders were. Some of the people who emerged as leaders were a surprise, and others who seemed to be strong leaders left the project. One woman attended all the meetings as the helping-hand volunteers were organizing, but she was very quiet and withdrawn. However, she became the consistent leader who recruited, trained and motivated volunteers and referred elderly who needed help.

Essential topics for all leadership training include: group management skills, including conflict resolution; methods of encouraging participation and group dynamics; organizational skills, including planning, delegation, fund-raising and budgeting; problem resolution, including problem identification and analysis; setting goals; group decision making; and evaluation skills, including assessment of results and revision of approaches. Leaders did emerge in the communities. Organizations such as BAMA KIDS now raise funds to hire project managers and to sustain volunteer activities in their community. They do strategic planning and evaluate their interventions.

Professionals and volunteers in successful partnerships remember to celebrate and laugh together. McKnight (1989) believes, "You will know that you are in a community if you often hear laughter and singing. You will know you are in an institution, corporation or bureaucracy if you hear the silence of long halls and reasoned meetings." Social events and celebrations are effective tools for building trust between health professionals and citizens and for recruiting volunteers. Every volunteer meeting in the rural Alabama project began with social chatter and food and ended with more food.

ATTRACTING VOLUNTEERS

It is easier to attract volunteers when there is a strong sense of need. The tradition of "neighbor helping neighbor," long recognized as a hallmark of rural life, formed the value base for the volunteer coalitions in the project. When people in the community learned that many elderly were not able to leave their homes, they volunteered to bring them groceries or take them to the doctor. When the community was shocked by the murder of a youth at a local grocery store, people formed the BAMA KIDS organization to mentor and tutor at risk young people.

People also volunteer when there is a strong sense of benefit either to themselves or the community. When people realize the changes that occur because of volunteer activity, it leads them to volunteer. Once momentum is established, the job of recruitment is easier. After houses were repaired and the elderly were assisted in the community, individuals came forward and asked how they could be involved in the volunteer activities. Volunteers are also attracted by learning and personal growth. One young, unemployed mother volunteered to assist the elderly after attending the home health aide class. She then studied and received a GED. Now she is employed as a teacher's assistant in the adult basic education program. She continues to volunteer.

VOLUNTEER RETENTION

In order to retain volunteers and to prevent burnout, it is necessary to provide orientation, training, education, and development and to create intrinsic rewards such as preparation for a job. Volunteers must feel prepared for the task and feel that what they contribute is valued. Volunteers do not provide cheap labor and may not save money. Training and development costs money.

Another way to retain volunteers is to foster the growth of personal relationships. Some of the volunteers in the Alabama project stated that they became a volunteer to help people, but a reason they continued was the enjoyment of the company of friends. One woman said, "I help Mr. and Mrs. Williams and I visit them every day. I enjoy this so much sometimes I stay for a week."

Celebrating the successes of volunteers is important to retention. Sometimes people volunteer year after year and no one ever recognizes them. We sponsored two or three community parties each year to thank volunteers and to celebrate progress. At these events, each volunteer was acknowledged and outstanding achievement was commended by special awards.

The consistent volunteers could articulate the benefits they received from volunteering. The treasurer of BAMA KIDS said that he benefited because he could measure and see progress. He said, "Children in BAMA KIDS perform at a higher level in schools than kids who are not. This gives me a sense of fulfillment." A minister said, "I have the ability to pass on knowledge to young men, knowledge I learned growing up hard in the streets." A mother said, "I am more responsible to my children and to my next door neighbor. Being involved has helped my children be more responsible for others." Another volunteer stated, "I feel better about myself because I can do for someone, especially children." A county commissioner who volunteered said, "Volunteering boosts my ego. I get a lot of satisfaction out of helping others.

Even though the project was able to build sustainable volunteer organizations, there were failures and barriers to success. When the project was implemented, many health and social service providers were skeptical about its chance to succeed. They did not recognize or respect the capacity of citizens to solve community problems and as John McKnight says, we emphasize the deficits (McKnight, 1987). A social service provider illustrated the attitude at the beginning of the project when he said, "These people don't care and they won't volunteer. They only want to receive services and welfare payments." One of the staff who was a resident of the county said that on the first day volunteers were to repair houses. She really didn't expect anyone to show up. She was surprised when forty men and women appeared on that cold morning and repaired ten homes.

Another barrier was the professionals' mode of thinking which emphasized the exclusive role of professionals to be both the service deliverers and the service providers. They did not want to share power and decision making with citizens or lose control and supervisory power over community-based programs. A social service professional was willing to support "using" volunteers to support the agency's programs but was not willing to include volunteers in planning and establishing priorities for the programs.

Some professionals from health and human service agencies who participated in the leadership training with volunteers, as well as participating as advisors and partners in the volunteers' programs, assisted in breaking down these barriers. They experienced the capacity of volunteers to make a difference. When they embraced the concepts of partnerships and shared decision making, they spread the word to their colleagues in the agencies. Slowly, agencies asked to participate in the activities. One service agency is replicating the model of professional-volunteer partnerships in other Alabama counties.

Nurses, traditionally committed to involving individuals in decision making, can play a key role in enabling citizens for participation in professional-volunteer partnerships. Nurses can provide leadership for professionals working in a new way with communities.

Even though building community partnerships can be difficult, it is rewarding work because professionals and volunteers participating in real partnerships lead to improvements in health and quality of life. The rewards are intrinsic because professionals must be committed to the community volunteers receiving praise for successes so they will feel ownership. I agree with my friend Ida George who assisted with community leadership development and wrote, "Successful organizers are those willing to enjoy the reflected glow of others' successes, those who find satisfaction, not in their own production, but in the production of others (1983, p. 42)."

References

Brudney, J.L. (1990). **Fostering volunteer programs in the public sector: Planning, initiating, and managing voluntary activities.** San Francisco: Jossey-Bass

Dewar, T. (1990). System talk turns off citizens. **Metro Monitor, 2(7),** 3.

Farley, S.S. (1997). Developing professional-community partnerships. In H. Grace and M. McCloskey (Eds.), **Current issues in nursing,** 5th edition (pp. 381-387). St. Louis: Mosby.

George, I.R. (1983). **Beyond promises: A guide for rural volunteer program development.** Montgomery, AL: Alabama Office of Voluntary Citizen Participation. State of Alabama Commission on Aging.

Hall-Russell, C., & Kasberg, R. (1997). **African-American traditions of giving and serving: A Midwest perspective.** Indianapolis: The Indiana University Center on Philanthropy.

Kretzmann, J.P., & McKnight, J.L. (1993). **Building communications from the inside out: A path toward finding and mobilizing a community's assets.** Evanston, IL: Center for Urban Affairs and Policy Research Neighborhood Innovations Network.

McKnight, J.L. (1987). Regenerating community. **Social Policy, 20(1),** 5015

Wasserbauer, L.I., Arrington, D.T. & Abraham, I.L. (1996). Using elderly volunteers to care for the elderly: Opportunities for nursing. **Nursing Economics, 14(4),** 232-237.

4

Service-Learning:

LESSONS FOR AND FROM NURSING

Robyn Gibboney, PhD

Nursing and the other health professions have a natural affinity for service-learning built into their educational systems because they have a long tradition of clinical training in community settings as an integral part of the curriculum. Nevertheless, nurse educators who have explicitly incorporated service-learning principles into their courses are emphatic that traditional nursing clinical courses in community settings are qualitatively different from service-learning community-based courses. In keeping with that perspective, there is a growing literature on how to relate service-learning to the health professions. Indeed, in 1995, the Pew Charitable Trusts and Corporation for National Service funded a project called Health Professions Schools in Service to the Nation (HPSISN), and out of that effort has grown an organization called the Community-Campus Partnerships for Health (CCPH). Together, these organizations and many others are dedicated to providing support for the integration of service-learning into the curricula for health professionals. The question I want to pose, however, is not simply how the principles of service-learning might enhance nursing education, but also how the values and practices of nursing might contribute to the burgeoning service-learning movement and how service-learning in nursing relates to the interface between nursing and philanthropy.

WHAT IS SERVICE-LEARNING?

Jane Norbeck (1997), one of the nursing editors for a series of discipline-based texts on service-learning being published in cooperation with the American Association of Higher Education (AAHE), notes that the definition of service-learning used by the Corporation for National and Community Service (1994) has two core elements: (a) service activities that meet community-defined needs; and (b) educational components that are structured to enhance critical thinking, group problem-solving competencies, and reflection on the service activities and community needs. She points out that service-learning not only connects theory with application and practice, but creates an environment where both the provider of the service and the recipient learn from each other and where there are opportunities for participants to explore the civic and social responsibilities of nursing education, practice and research.

Bringle and Hatcher (1996) define service-learning as "a credit-bearing experience in which students participate in an organized service activity that meets needs identified by the local community, and then reflect on the service activity to gain further understanding of course content, a broader appreciation of the discipline, and an enhanced sense of civic responsibility" (p. 222). Although the Corporation for National and Community Service and many institutions endorse co-curricular and curriculum-based service-learning, it is significant that Bringle and Hatcher's definition explicitly requires integrating service experiences into academic courses. This approach is also endorsed by the HPSISN evaluation team. Their preliminary report notes that "experiences designed as 'add on' activities have ... diminished benefit" (Gelmon et al., 1997).

Proponents claim that "service, combined with learning, adds value to each and transforms both ... [so that together they contribute to] the common good" (Giles, Honnet, & Migliore, 1991, p. 24). In many ways, however, this "new" pedagogy is not new at all. Service-learning builds on many older traditions in higher education, among them: (a) the service part of higher education's teaching-research-service tripartite mission; (b) experiential education; and (c) a commitment to encouraging student development. Van Til and

Ledwig (1995) suggest four possible roots for the service-learning movement: (a) the social activism of the 1960s; (b) Dewey's advocacy for experiential education; (c) Dewey's promotion of education-community ties; and (d) the tradition of voluntary action and civic participation necessary in a democratic society. They argue that for the general citizenry, the fourth may be the most compelling reason to support service-learning opportunities, and organizations like the National Society for Experiential Education (NSEE), HPSISN and CCPH stress the importance of building strong, mutually beneficial partnerships; however, most educators tend to stress the movement's ties to Dewey and experiential education (Giles & Eyler, 1994), realizing that colleagues are unlikely to risk involvement in the movement unless they are convinced it is sound pedagogy. Further, Zlotkowski (1996) cites Levine's observation that "student volunteer movements tend to be a passing phenomenon in higher education, rising and falling on campuses roughly every 30 years" (p. 21) and argues that the way for service-learning to avoid this "periodic mortality" (p. 22) is for it to be linked closely to the stability of the faculty's teaching mission. To the extent that nursing education and practice have historically been linked to the community more than many disciplines, nurses are well positioned to provide leadership in institutionalizing a commitment to service that is linked to learning.

Existing Models of Service-Learning

Robert Sigmon, who helped pioneer service-learning in the late 1970s, has developed a typology for service-learning that stresses the importance of balancing service and learning as well as the core value of reciprocity (**Table 1**). He describes four broad categories for the different approaches to combining service and learning:

Table 1. Typology for Service-Learning (Sigmon, 1994).	
service-LEARNING	Learning goals primary; service outcomes secondary
SERVICE-learning	Service outcomes primary; learning goals secondary
service-learning	Service and learning goals completely separate
SERVICE-LEARNING	Service and learning goals of equal weight and each enhances the other for all participants

Using this typology, Furco (1996) developed a model that depicts a continuum for service-learning in the context of voluntary action and experiential education generally (**Figure 1**). He stresses that where a particular service/education program lies on the continuum "is determined by its *primary intended beneficiary* and its overall *balance between service and learning*" (p. 3). According to this model, traditional approaches to nursing clinicals would probably fall under field education, where the emphasis is on the learning acquired by the provider (i.e., the nursing student), though there are also strong intentions to benefit the recipients of the service (i.e., real nursing care is provided to the client). What service-learning attempts to do is balance who benefits and increase understanding of the context so that the relationship is more reciprocal.

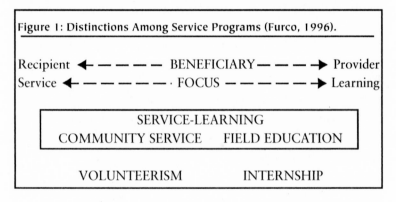

Figure 1: Distinctions Among Service Programs (Furco, 1996).

Recipient ◄ — — — — BENEFICIARY — — — ➤ Provider
Service ◄ — — — — — · FOCUS — — — — — ➤ Learning

SERVICE-LEARNING
COMMUNITY SERVICE   FIELD EDUCATION

VOLUNTEERISM   INTERNSHIP

Other models of service-learning stress other aspects of the experience. For example, the service-learning model developed by Delve, Mintz, and Stewart (1990) links service-learning outcomes to the student development theories of Gilligan (1982), Kohlberg (1981) and Perry (1970). The model assumes that students move along a continuum from charity to justice as they progress through five stages of development: Phase 1 - Exploration; Phase 2 - Clarification; Phase 3 - Realization; Phase 4 - Activation; and Phase 5 - Internalization. The implication is that direct, one-to-one interactions (seen as typical of Phase 2 or 3) are at a lower stage of moral and intellectual development than advocacy for social change (seen as typical of Phase 5). Delve et al. also suggest that the goal of the service-learning educator is to help students move away from charity and become more committed to social justice.

Kendall (1990), too, sees social justice as preferable to charity. In distinguishing between service-learning and community service without a formal learning component, she identifies two key factors: (a) service-learning explicitly includes features that foster participants' learning about the larger social issues behind the human needs to which they are responding, including the historical, sociological, cultural and political contexts; it should help students see their participation in the *larger context of social justice and policy rather than charity* [italics added]; and (b) service-learning places an emphasis on reciprocity — that is, the exchange of both giving and receiving between the server and the served is a way to *minimize the traditionally paternalistic approach to service* [italics added] (p. 20).

Barber (1992) also supports a social justice approach. He maintains that service should promote an understanding of how private interest and public good are linked; that service should be seen as a condition of citizenship rather than a form of altruism, because "the language of charity drives a wedge between self-interest and altruism, leading students to believe that service is a matter of sacrificing private interests to moral virtue ... [whereas] the language of citizenship suggests that self-interests are always embedded in communities of action and that in serving neighbors one also serves oneself" (p. 249).

Barber and Battistoni (1993) contend that the primary justification for service programs in higher education should be pedagogical and that the goal of service-learning should be to nurture citizenship and the students' understanding of the interdependence of individuals in communities. Contrasting what they call a "philanthropic framework" with a civic one, they suggest that service as philanthropy can be captured by the statement: "I am obliged to help others less fortunate than myself, and it will do my character good to do so!" A civic perspective, on the other hand, is captured by the statement: "I cannot flourish unless the communities to which I belong flourish, and it is in my (enlightened) self-interest to become a responsible member of those communities — whether they are my school, my neighborhood, or my nation." The emphasis in this model is on the service provider's rationale for involvement, but the rationale is shaped by a very limited notion of philanthropy. There is no recognition of the many motivations, goals and approaches encompassed by philanthropy broadly defined as "voluntary action for the public good" (Payton, 1988).

More recently, Morton (1995) has challenged the assumptions underlying the models proposed by Delve et al. (1990), Kendall (1990) and Barber (1992). He rejects the idea of a hierarchical continuum from charity to social justice; instead, he views service in the context of three "ranges" or paradigms, which he labels charity, program and social change — all of which would fall within the broader conceptualization of philanthropy. Each paradigm reflects a unique world view and implies different kinds of relationships. According to Morton's model, service-learning is a way for individuals to achieve greater depth in their understanding and commitment to service in any one of the three paradigms. Given students' already established preferences, he argues, educators should not so much seek to change a student's paradigm — for example, from charity to social change — as encourage students to self-consciously name and work more consistently within the paradigm for service that best fits their basic world view. According to Morton:

> Only occasionally ... is a primary orientation given up for an alternative.
> ... While we can do work across these paradigms, we are most at home
> in one or another, and interpret what we do according to the standards
> of the one in which we are most at home ... And, done well, ... all three
> [paradigms] lead ultimately toward the transformation of an individual
> within a community, and toward the transformation of the communities
> themselves. (p. 29)

PRINCIPLES OF GOOD PRACTICE

Bearing in mind the goals and values of service-learning, the NSEE initiated and coordinated a conference in Racine, Wisconsin, to develop principles for good practice in combining service and learning. Known as the Wingspread principles (Honnet & Poulsen, 1989), these guidelines (Table 2) emphasize the importance of building and sustaining relationships that are mutually satisfying — because all parties recognize the value of clearly defined goals, responsibilities, preparation, support and evaluation — and that serve as the foundation for structured opportunities to provide real service, reflect on that service and adapt to changing circumstances.

Table 2. Wingspread Principles of Good Practice (Honnet & Poulson, 1989)

An effective and sustained program that combines service and learning:

1. Engages people in responsible and challenging actions for the common good.
2. Provides structured opportunities for people to reflect critically on their service experience.
3. Articulates clear service and learning goals for everyone involved.
4. Allows for those with needs to define those needs.
5. Clarifies the responsibilities of each person and organization involved.
6. Matches service providers and service needs through a process that recognizes changing circumstances.
7. Expects genuine, active and sustained organizational commitment.
8. Includes training, supervision, monitoring, support, recognition and evaluation to meet service and learning goals.
9. Ensures that the time commitment for service and learning is flexible, appropriate and in the best interests of all involved.
10. Is committed to program participation by and with diverse populations.

Building on the Wingspread principles, Howard (1993) articulated how these more general guidelines might be interpreted from a faculty perspective. Howard stresses faculty involvement in embedding the service opportunities within credit-bearing courses, concern for academic integrity and development of criteria for assessing learning outcomes. He also notes how the role of the faculty member must be reconceptualized as the arena for learning shifts from an information-assimilation model, where faculty are in control, to an experiential model, where faculty are facilitators and "harvesters" who attempt to identify clear criteria and mechanisms for learning but must also be prepared for uncertainty and variation.

Mintz and Hesser (1996) point out that service-learning involves "working in a creative tension marked by collaboration, reciprocity, and diversity ... within the context of the interrelationships among three domains or partners" (p. 34) — the academy, the students and the community. They suggest using the metaphor of a kaleidoscope to describe how the shifting emphases among all these variables can create a wide variety of programs and outcomes. How a particular service/education project is viewed depends on the extent to which the collaboration among the three is genuine, the degree of reciprocity in the relationship, and the level at which inherent differences influence the process.

In summary, there is a growing literature on the nature of service-learning in which the differences between service-learning and other types of experiential education are articulated, as well as the goals, values and principles of practice that should guide efforts to link service with learning in an academic setting. Ideally, service-learning contrasts with the "ugly academic" model that has all too often typified relationships between higher education institutions and the communities in which they are located — that is, a paternalistic or exploitative use of communities by the academy, where "experts" descend on "the unfortunate" to teach them what they ought to know, or outsiders come to gather information (e.g., another needs assessment or data for a research project) but never act on what they find out to make a difference in the lives of those who provided the information. Further, service-learning advocates claim that service-learning can increase students' understanding of course objectives, heighten their awareness of civic responsibility, encourage personal and cognitive development, and lead to the transformation of communities by creating partnerships and strengthening relationships among different constituencies in communities where institutions of higher education are located. If these claims are true — and a growing body of literature is beginning to support them — then educators in a field like nursing, which has a long tradition of service in and to communities beyond the academy, should be among those who see the value of this approach and therefore serve as advocates for service-learning.

SERVICE-LEARNING IN NURSING: EXPANDING TRADITIONAL VALUES

Sarena Seifer, director of HPSISN, claims that the nurses involved in the HPSISN project were among the first to "get it" — that is, because nursing has historically been and continues to be a provider of service and advocate for quality care, extending the vision for health to communities as well as individuals, service-learning principles and practices were understood and incorporated into nursing curricula more readily than into the curricula for other health professions. In fact, 15 of the 19 HPSISN-funded programs, many of which are interdisciplinary, involved nursing — more than any other discipline in the health sciences (Table 3). Still, according to Norbeck

(1997), "nursing as a profession within academic, research, and health care organizations has not, until recently, begun to embrace true service-learning" (p. 1). This section will explore why and how nursing is making this transition.

Seifer points out that changes in health care delivery have created an environment where there is "a growing demand for the skills of collaboration, effective communication, and teamwork" (Seifer, Mutha, & Connors, 1996, p. 36). She also suggests that service-

Table 3. Discipline Involvement in HPSISN-Funded Projects		
Nursing (Includes nurse practitioner)	15	projects
Allopathic Medicine (Includes physician assistant)	11	projects
Dentistry	7	projects
Pharmacy	6	projects
Public Health	5	projects
Social Work, Osteopathic Medicine, Health Administration, Fitness & Nutrition	1	project each

learning is an effective way to develop the competencies called for by the Pew Health Professions Commission (O'Neil, 1993) — competencies such as practicing prevention, promoting healthy lifestyles, and involving patients and their families in health care decision-making, which nursing stressed even before the current shifts in health care delivery to community-based settings and managed care models. In addition, Seifer sees service-learning as a way to address many of the deficiencies in training that health professionals report (Shugars, O'Neil, & Bader, 1991) — deficiencies such as responding to the needs of different cultural and ethnic groups; understanding and supporting the role of community service agencies; and ensuring access to quality health care for all segments of the population, all of which are more apparent as hospitals and agencies move towards integrated systems of care.

The AAHE monograph on nursing and service-learning, edited by Norbeck, Connolly, & Koerner (1997), provides a series of essays on theoretical issues; case studies on specific service-learning programs and experiences, which offer insights on practical issues involved in planning and implementing service-learning; and relevant tools, such as syllabi, assignments and student projects, as well as an annotated bibliography and a list of resource persons to assist those interested in initiating a service-learning component.

CCPH (Seifer & Connors, 1997) also has published a monograph that describes not only a number of exemplary models for how nursing has incorporated service-learning into the curriculum but also interdisciplinary and multi-institutional models for service-learning, where nursing is frequently a major player. Service-learning programs in nursing education include the following:

- The School-Linked Community Partnership Program of the University of Maryland delivers community-based care through a nurse-managed clinic at the School of Nursing, seven school-based clinics and a "Wellmobile" (a school-linked mobile health unit) in partnership with various public and private agencies such as a managed care organization, two health departments, several school districts and numerous private organizations. Outcomes include institutions' awareness of the need to cross lines of authority not usually bridged in the past, students' greater understanding of the autonomous care nurses can provide, and increases in students' willingness to be open-minded about populations and communities they had never before experienced.

- The community health course for nursing students at the University of Washington focuses on community health assessment; community organizing to develop partnerships, coalitions and forums for advocacy to promote community health; developing health programs in response to health concerns identified by the community through analysis of community health characteristics, capacities and resources; and the effect of national, state and local health policies on the health of communities. Students work with a wide variety of community-based organizations. One program success was the church federation's adoption of a year-long health promotion program that addressed health concerns identified in collaboration with a predominantly African-American church. The program incorporated the congregation's cultural beliefs and meaningful Bible scriptures.

Nursing's leadership in interdisciplinary service-learning includes the work of Beverly Flynn, director of the Institute of Action Research for Community Health at Indiana University School of Nursing, in facilitating a "Health of the Public" program. The goal of the project was to develop an interdisciplinary seminar focused on population-based health care concepts, community issues that impact on health, and skill development for facilitating community problem resolution. Participants in the project have noted that "community-based, interdisciplinary action research requires shifts in attitudes and ways of working as co-equals and collaborators rather than in departmentalized and hierarchical formats" (Seifer and Connors, 1997, p. 110). Moreover, this collaborative model calls for more than teamwork among health professionals; it also entails seeing each community partner as a "full and valued participant in the process of empowering the community to develop strategies for improving health" (p. 110).

Nursing also provides leadership in the "Redirecting Health Professions Education Toward Community-based Primary Care" project. The project is implemented through the Center for Community Health, Education, Research and Service, a partnership involving the Northeastern College of Nursing, Boston University School of Medicine, Boston Medical Center, Boston City Department of Health and Hospitals, and twelve community health centers. Experiences are integrated throughout students' degree programs and coordinated through the system of Academic Community Health Centers (analogous to teaching hospitals, but based in community facilities), whose governing board has majority representation from health centers and community residents (68%) rather than academic personnel. Nursing's commitment to this project is evident in the 100% participation rate among BSN nursing students, compared with 28% participation for medical students. The success of the program is evident in high levels of student satisfaction and retention, as well as career choices among students who have participated in the program over a four-year program of study. Among nursing students who could be contacted, 38% had positions in community settings, although only 17% had indicated interest in a community-based career upon entering nursing school; and 65% of graduating medical students who participated went into primary care residencies, compared with only 32% of non-participating medical students.

To some, these programs may not seem significantly different from

LORETTE WILMOT LIBRARY
NAZARETH COLLEGE

traditional clinicals for community health nursing courses. However, the HPSISN preliminary evaluation report emphasizes the importance of helping health professions educators distinguish between traditional clinicals and course work that uses a service-learning orientation: "Many faculty still are confused about the distinction between service-learning and other community-based experiential placements. The difficulty appears to lie in distinguishing the concept of service to address community needs and respond to community assets, as compared with addressing clinical problems through provision of health services" (Gelmon et al., 1997, p. v). Indeed, HPSISN found that:

> The transformational impact of service-learning on students was far more evident at sites where the service-learning was truly course-based, required, and did not involve an exclusive focus on community-based clinical work. Students were strongly affected by working with individuals in non-clinical settings where they could learn about the daily context of individuals' lives, and experience the complex and fragile network of support services on which they depend. This awareness of the challenges of ordinary life experienced by potential clients led to the greatest transformation of student views of the role of service in their profession. Service-learning in clinical settings can be valuable but is almost always overwhelmed by issues of clinical skill development and application. (p. iv)

What is it, then, that distinguishes service-learning from clinical training? Seifer (personal communication) suggests the following:

- Balance between service and learning objectives in order to foster citizenship rather than clinical skill development. (Though clinical skill development may also be an outcome, there is equal attention to developing critical thinking, group problem-solving competencies, and reflection on service activities, community needs, and the socioeconomic influences on health.)

- Responding to community-identified concerns. (This requires that the role of community organizations be integral, so that community organizations are seen as equal partners in the service-learning experience and not simply as sites with clients in need of health care, which provide opportunities for clinical skill development.) In order for nursing students to grasp these concepts and develop the skills needed to achieve such broad goals, reflection on the context for the service must be included, and an openness to learn from community members — not just provide nursing care to them — must be promoted.

A Two-Way Exchange

While there is a growing literature that addresses questions about how service-learning can enhance health professions education, including nursing, questions about how nursing might enhance service-learning are only beginning to be explored. Evaluators for the HPSISN project identified the following key student outcomes for service-learning in the health professions (including, but not limited to, nursing students): awareness of community needs; understanding of health policy and its implications; awareness of socioeconomic, environmental and cultural determinants of health; development of leadership skills; commitment to service; career choice; sensitivity to diversity; involvement with community; and personal and professional development. Using these criteria, HPSISN has sought to measure the impact of service-learning not only on students but also on the institution as a whole, on the faculty and on the community partners.

What is striking about the list of outcomes is the extent to which it echoes outcomes that many nursing programs have long sought to achieve. For example, before Indiana University School of Nursing had considered service-learning as a particular pedagogy, the faculty had endorsed the following values as the foundation for their teaching, research and service: responsibility for health promotion, disease prevention and health restoration; emphasis on facilitating the "whole person"; encouragement of self-help; concern for the relationship between people and their environment(s); sensitivity to cultural diversity; understanding of global health care issues; importance of continuity of care; development, testing and evaluation of innovative practice models; and influencing and participating in health care systems development and reform. Assuming that IU's nursing faculty reflect values held broadly by nurse educators, what might we discover about the relationship between nursing and service-learning that could shed light on the nature of the kind of service toward which philanthropy in general strives? What is it about nursing that promotes "voluntary action for the public good" (Payton, 1988)? What can service-learning educators in other disciplines learn from the way nursing has incorporated service-learning into the curriculum? To begin to discover answers to these questions, the nature of nursing practice must be explored.

In her book describing nursing at the Beth Israel Hospital in Boston, Suzanne Gordon (1997) cites a study in which researchers at the Harvard Medical School conducted telephone interviews of a random sample consisting of 298 nurse practitioners and 501 internists, family practice physicians and general practice physicians. They asked participants to tell them what they would do in the following case:

> A man you have never seen before comes to your office seeking help for intermittent sharp epigastric [stomach] pains that are relieved by meals but are worse on an empty stomach. The patient has just moved from out of state and brings along a report of an endoscopy performed a month ago showing diffuse gastritis of moderate severity, but no ulcer. Is there a particular therapy you would choose at that point, or would you need additional information? (p. 101)

Gordon reports that 95% of the physicians (twice as many physicians as nurse practitioners) would have initiated treatment without seeking additional information, in contrast with 80% of nurse practitioners initiating treatment only after seeking additional information. Those who asked for additional information would have learned that medications currently used were two aspirins four times daily for stomach pain, that the patient's son was killed in a car accident six weeks earlier, that he drank five cups of coffee per day, had only one large meal daily at lunch, smoked two packs of cigarettes per day, and had two cocktails with lunch and two glasses of wine at night. Without the additional information, 63% of the physicians would have prescribed medication, whereas most of the nurse practitioners recommended a change in diet, counseling and trying to deal with the patient's heavy use of aspirin, coffee, cigarettes and alcohol (Safriet, 1986, cited in Gordon, 1997, p. 102).

Gordon (1997) also recounts numerous instances where nurses promoted interdisciplinary teamwork and demonstrated highly developed competence in problem-solving and critical thinking; communication and networking skills; understanding of cultural, ethical, political and legal issues; professional activism; and managing complex situations. Just as Lillian Wald was faced with the reality of poverty in New York's tenements in 1883, and because of her encounters "moved beyond a charitable to a social agenda by insisting that illness and poverty are inseparable," so nurses today are part of health care teams that cover the full spectrum of care, from intensive care units to home health services, and are trained not only to manage symptoms associated with disease but also address aspects of the environment that may be affecting the patient's quality of life.

Throughout her book, Gordon documents nursing's holistic approach to health care — which is person-focused, as opposed to disease-focused — as well as the important role that nurses play in ensuring the quality of care. Through my own interaction with nurses during the seven years I have been associated with the Indiana University School of Nursing, I have seen this perspective emphasized over and over again. Further, nursing's goals of empowerment and maximizing functional abilities contrast with medicine's goals of eradicating disease; indeed, nursing's goals remind me of McKnight's (1989) framework for community development. He argues that service systems build on people's deficiencies, whereas communities build on people's capacities. According to McKnight, bureaucracy is not the problem; the problem is that money goes to health and human service professionals instead of the individuals in traditionally under-served communities who come to depend on various services. To illustrate his point, he contrasts his experiences in organizing block clubs on the west side of Chicago with an "anti-poverty program" where experts doing a survey might have characterized a woman as "dropout, two years" instead of "educated ten years," and placed emphasis on her illiteracy, need for glasses, and support of two teenage daughters and their children (providing the rationale for a service center staffed by GED trainers, reading tutors, a neighborhood optometrist, and teenage pregnancy counselors) rather than on the woman's ability to "take charge" when a neighbor's child was hit by a car or tell people whom to call when a tree fell down across the street. In other words, the anti-poverty program experts saw this woman as needy, while her neighbors saw her as "the leader on the block."

A Comparison of Nursing and
Service-Learning's Values and Practices

Nursing has been defined as helping people do for themselves what they would do unaided if they had the knowledge, skills and resources. Service-learning has been defined as a credit-bearing experience in which students participate in an organized service activity that meets needs identified by the local community, and then reflect on the service activity to gain further understanding of course content, a broader appreciation of the discipline, and an enhanced sense of civic responsibility. **Table 4** depicts how the values and practices of these two fields are related. Because nurses have a long tradition of building relationships with patients and their families in order to

Table 4: Comparison of Values and Practices	
Nursing	**Service-Learning**
Holistic approach (meeting the biological, psychological, social and spiritual needs of the patient, family or community)	Reflection to increase understanding of the context for service activities (in addition to providing the service)
Person-focused, not disease-focused; emphasis on empowerment and maximizing functional abilities to enhance quality of life	Emphasis on discovering capacities/assets in the community and on incorporating them into collaborative relationships to enhance quality of life
Focus on the fit between person/group and environment; importance of cultural sensitivity	Meeting real community needs that are defined by the community; importance of partnerships and reciprocity
Systems framework for problem-solving; nurse as part of a health care team	Valuing of interdisciplinary collaboration and increased understanding of civic responsibility (i.e., the role of the individual in the community)
Valuing of research utilization (i.e., nursing research defined as finding answers to important clinical questions and putting that knowledge to practical use)	Valuing of participatory action research and inclusion of community partners in evaluations of service-learning experiences as well as assessment of community assets and needs

effectively manage patient care, they have often been seen as bridges that offer access to a wide array of health services. For example, at the two Shalom Wellness Clinics, which provide nurse-managed care in church settings to under-served populations in Indianapolis, there are countless stories of clients who have benefitted from the clinics but were receiving no previous regular health care before that. For a variety of reasons (e.g., lack of insurance, lack of adequate transportation, lack of trust, etc.), many individuals and families in these communities were outside the traditional health care system. Bridging that gap and opening doors are the nurses at the Shalom Wellness Clinics. As health professionals in the community, they are modeling — for students, colleagues and community partners — the reciprocal relationships advocated by service-learning. Moreover, not only have residents in the neighborhoods near the clinics received health care services previously denied them, but the nurses are helping to address larger issues facing the community. Together, the community and the clinics demonstrate the meaning of voluntary action for the public good and the kind of socialization needed for service-learning — in any discipline — to reflect the ideals of collaboration, reciprocity and increased understanding of civic responsibility.

IMPLICATIONS OF SERVICE-LEARNING
IN NURSING FOR PHILANTHROPY

Because the purpose of this conference is to explore the interface between nursing and philanthropy, I would like to conclude this presentation with some additional thoughts on how service-learning in nursing can shed light on our understanding of voluntary action for the public good. How to effectively transmit the philanthropic tradition to individuals is central to the concerns of nonprofits and voluntary action, for without volunteers and donors, they cannot survive. Further, as health professionals struggle to deal with changes in the health care delivery system, which many fear is increasingly driven by concern for the bottom line rather than quality care, it becomes all the more imperative that providers espouse a service ethic.

Quality care is not the only outcome at risk, however. Barber (1992) claims that unless the value of service is impressed upon succeeding generations, our democratic way of life is in danger. He echoes the concerns of Putnam (1995), who warns against declining "social capital," and Bellah et al. (1986), who lament Americans' preoccupation with individualism and the way our definitions of success, freedom and justice are shaped by personal, rather than communal, values. Service-learning proponents claim that combining service and learning is an effective way to teach students about both their role in community and their role in a democratic society, and suggest that service-learning is therefore a possible antidote to the apathy and egoism plaguing society today.

Although not everyone agrees (e.g., critics like Boyte [1991] suggest that "community service ... teaches little about the arts of participation in public life" [p. 765] because young people often see service as an alternative to politics, not as training for it), there is a growing body of literature that links commitment to community and civic mindedness with service-learning experiences. For example, in my dissertation research on a group of non-nurses who shared a service-learning experience, I found that many participants viewed service, self and community as interrelated in a cycle of change, which can at the same time affect individual service providers, individual service recipients and broader social issues. This circular image of the relationship among philanthropic acts prompted them to question the hierarchical models for service-learning, which urge educators to move students from charity to social justice. Rather, like Morton (1995), participants in the study accepted a variety of service experiences as valid — from one-on-one acts of kindness, typically characterized as charity, to advocacy for changes in policy, typically seen as social justice.

Similarly, the rejection of hierarchical structures in health care has implications for nurses. Just as real service-learning requires that the academy see the community as collaborative partners rather than as needy recipients of the academy's expertise or subjects in a research project, so must health care see all health providers as valued members of an interdisciplinary team. And just as many of the

HPSISN-funded service-learning projects cut across disciplines, so must education for all health professionals socialize students into working collaboratively to achieve high quality care and broad access to health services.

Despite the fact that the "voluntary" part of the definition for philanthropy is problematic if the service is a required part of a required course, service-learning is certainly related to philanthropy in that those participating in this pedagogical approach are providing service or action for the public good. Within the health professions, this good is "public" rather than simply for the learners themselves to the extent that the service is meeting real needs identified by the community and not just providing opportunities in a community-based setting for students to practice clinical skills. However, providing service through a credit-bearing course is only the beginning of service-learning. Like nurses who seek to understand why a health condition exists and how to enhance the quality of life for patients, their families and the communities in which they live, service-learners must search below the surface to discover why the community needs the service provided, and service-learning facilitators (both faculty and community partners) must be willing to expand their notion of civic involvement.

A FINAL WORD

In a recent issue of the *Boston Globe* (June 18, 1996), the following parable appeared in a column by James Carroll as part of a tribute to Kip Tiernan:

> What would you do if you saw a baby floating helpless in a river? You'd rescue it. And if other babies came floating down? You'd get help, and you'd rescue those babies, too. If more and more babies kept coming down the river, you would organize rescue squads and foster homes. But at what point would your gaze turn upstream, and when would rage choke you with the question, "Who is throwing babies in the river?" And what would you do then?

The parable illustrates the dilemma faced by service providers — where should we place our priorities? How can we work together to save the babies who are in the river already but also look upstream to discover why so many babies are in the river and figure out what we can do to change the situation? Educators, researchers and health providers alike must reject a hierarchical view of charity and justice in favor of a more integrated concept, and must see all of the health disciplines as integral parts of a health care system designed to treat not only disease (problems/needs) but also address health promotion, disease prevention and aspects of the environment that affect quality of life. We must be conscious of the whole range of service, and encourage our students and colleagues in the health professions to "self-consciously name and work more consistently within the paradigm for service that best fits their basic world view" (Morton, 1995, p. 31); and to serve in such a way that they are always aware of the dignity of the service recipients, who, true to service-learning's emphasis on reciprocity, are not only service recipients but also service providers. As one of my former students remarked, the more we, as a society, are commited to serving each other, the less we will need to worry about broader issues of social justice, for a society that models true charity — not in the sense of giving hand-outs but in the sense of voluntary action for the public good — will be a just society.

References

Barber, B. R., & Battistoni, R. (1993). A season of service: Introducing service learning into the liberal arts curriculum. **Political Science & Politics, 26(2),** 235-236.

Bellah, R. N., & Associates. (1986). Habits of the heart: Individualism and commitment in American life. New York: Harper & Row.

Boyte, H. C. (1991). Community service and civic education. **Phi Delta Kappan, 72,** 765-767.

Bringle, R., & Hatcher, J. (1996). Implementing service learning into higher education. **Journal of Higher Education, 67(2),** 221-239.

Corporation for National and Community Service. (1994). **Grant application guidelines for Learn and Serve America: Higher education.** Washington, DC: Author.

Delve, C., Mintz, S., & Stewart, G. (Eds.). (1990). **Community service as values education.** San Francisco: Jossey-Bass.

Eyler, J., Giles, D., & Schmiede, A. (1996). **A practitioner's guide to reflection in service-learning.** Nashville, TN: Vanderbilt University.

Furco, A. (1996). Service-learning: a balanced approach to experiential education. **Expanding boundaries: service and learning,** Vol. 1. New York, NY: The Corporation for national service learn and serve America: higher education.

Gelmon, S., Holland, B., Driscoll, A., Morris, B., & Shinnamon, A. (1997). Health Professions Schools in Service to the Nation (HPSISN) preliminary evaluation. San Francisco: Center for the Health Professions at the University of California-San Francisco.

Giles, D., & Eyler, J. (1994). The theoretical roots of service-learning in John Dewey: Toward a theory of service-learning. **Michigan Journal of Community Service Learning, 1,** 77-85.

Gilligan, C. (1982). **In a different voice: Psychological theory and women's development.** Cambridge, MA: Harvard University Press.

Gordon, S. (1997). **Life support: Three nurses on the front lines.** Boston: Little, Brown and Co.

Honnet, E., & Poulsen, S. (1989). Principles of good practice for combining service and learning. **Wingspread special report.** Racine, WI: The Johnson Foundation, Inc.

Howard, J. (1993). Community service learning in the curriculum. In J. Howard (Ed.), **Praxis I: A faculty casebook on community service learning** (pp. 3-12). Ann Arbor, MI: OCSL Press, University of Michigan.

Kendall, J. C. (Ed.). (1990). **Combining service and learning: A resource book for community and public service,** Vol. 1. Raleigh, NC: National Society for Internships and Experiential Education.

Kohlberg, L. (1981). **The philosophy of moral development: Moral stages and the idea of justice.** San Francisco: Harper and Row.

McKnight, J. (1989). Why "servanthood" is bad. **The Other Side, 25(1),** 38-40.

Mintz, S. & Hesser, G. (1996). Principles of good practice in service learning. In B. Jacoby (Ed.), **Service learning in higher education.** San Francisco: Jossey-Bass.

Morton, K. (1995). The irony of service: Charity, project, and social change in service-learning. **Michigan Journal on Community Service Learning, 2(1),** 19-32.

Norbeck, J., Connolly, C., & Koerner, J. (1998). **Caring and community: Concepts and models for service-learning in nursing.** Washington, DC: American Association of Higher Education.

O'Neil, E. (1993). **Health professions education for the future: Schools in service to the nation.** San Francisco: Pew Health Professions Commission.

Payton, R. L. (1988). **Philanthropy: Voluntary action for the public good.** New York: American Council on Education/Macmillan.

Perry, W. G. (1970). **Forms of intellectual and ethical development in the college years.** New York: Holt, Rinehart, and Winston.

Putnam, R. D. (1995). Bowling alone: America's declining social capital. **Journal of Democracy, 6(1),** 65-78.

Seifer, S., & Connors, K. (1997). **A guide for developing community-responsive models in health professions education.** San Francisco: Community-Campus Partnerships for Health.

Seifer, S.D., et al. (1996). Service learning in health professions education: Barriers, facilitators, and strategies for success. In **Expanding boundaries: serving and learning** (pp. 36-41). Washington, DC: Corporation for National Service.

Shugars, D., O'Neil, E., & Bader, J. (1991). **Survey of practitioners' perceptions of their education**. Durham, NC: Pew Health Professions Commission.

Sigmon, R. (1994). Serving to learn, learning to serve. **Linking service with learning**. Washington, DC: Council of Independent Colleges.

Van Til, J., & Ledwig, F. (1995). National service: Twenty questions and some answers. In T. D. Connors (Ed.), **The volunteer management handbook** (pp. 361-378). New York: Wiley.

---

[1]Service-learning is "a method under which students or participants learn and develop through active participation in thoughtfully organized service that is conducted in and meets the needs of a community and is coordinated with an elementary school, secondary school, institution of higher education, or community service program, and with the community; helps foster civic responsibility; is integrated into and enhances the academic curriculum of the student's program or the educational components of the community service program in which the participants are enrolled; and includes structured time for the students and participants to reflect on the service experience."

5

Private Support for Nursing
WHAT IS THE PHILANTHROPIC APPEAL

Joyce J. Fitzpatrick

I wish to congratulate the organizers of this conference. The topic is timely and relevant to the values and goals of professional nursing. I am honored to have been asked to present the paper for this plenary session on the philanthropic appeal of nursing. And I applaud the conference visionary, Dr. Angela McBride, for recognizing that this topic captured two areas of thinking that have been near and dear to my heart, my thinking and my professional activity for the past 15 years. First of all I have spent a great deal of time conceptualizing the nature of nursing, writing about our disciplinary structure and need to define our domain of science and practice. On the more practical side, as a dean of a private school of nursing in a major research university where the "every tub on its own bottom" philosophy is the bible, I have spent most of my time translating the nature of nursing to many stake holders, funders and potential funders. I have met with countless individual donors, corporate CEOs, foundation program staff, and foundation and corporate board members; all of these meetings were focused on finding a meaningful fit between the goals of our school and potential funders. Over the years I have learned a great deal — and most of all I have learned that we, as professional nurses, have a great story to tell.

I have been asked to focus my remarks today on the conceptual appeal of nursing. Thus, this is not a presentation on the techniques of development or fund raising. Yet, implicit in my comments are some lessons to be learned, some tips for translating nursing to the philanthropist.

Let me first state my bias...that is, the very core of the art of professional nursing...the commitment to humanity...the commitment to others less healthy or less fortunate due to poverty, illness, or other human conditions...is the same driving force for philanthropy, which is by definition an act of goodwill toward others, a concern for others, expressed through generosity. Across the globe, from country to country, many of nursing's roots can be traced to the religious, many of the others can be traced to the philanthropists, for the nurses often are the messenger, the vehicle for the translation of the philanthropists' wishes to make the world a better place.

Having recently traveled the globe and given a number of speeches in countries where English is not the primary spoken language, I have had many experiences with language translators, those responsible for the simultaneous translation of many carefully crafted speeches into a language that is understood by the participants, a language where words and dialects, and even intonations, may have different cultural meanings. And for this presentation today, I want to use the metaphor of the language translator to understand the conceptual fit between nursing and philanthropy. For in my fund raising experience I have found that most often the public has little awareness of what nursing is and what nurses do. As a group, nurses are not only invisible but they also are self effacing, not used to public negotiating, innovation or entrepreneurship. Nurses are not used to seizing public power or control.

First in this presentation I will try to outline for you the conceptual congruence between nursing and philanthropy. Then, I will share with you some success stories that illustrate the congruence. I hope the principal dimensions are evident in the stories, and I trust that our respondents will add to our deliberations. Most of all, I look forward to the interaction period, when together we can advance our understandings.

UNDERSTANDINGS OF NURSING

Florence Nightingale: The Legend.

All nurses throughout the globe are familiar with the Mother of Modern Nursing: Florence Nightingale. The history of Nightingale, the woman, the nurse, and the scientist is a complex one. On August 10, 1910, two days after her death, *The New York Times* stated, "Few lives have been more useful or more inspiring than hers."

Florence was born into a wealthy family on May 12, 1820, while her family was on extended vacation in Florence, Italy. In spite of her family's wealth and social standing, Florence showed an early concern for the suffering and poverty of others. She has been described as a perfectionist, a somewhat morbid child, who never seemed to be satisfied with herself. Throughout her life she was driven to improve herself and the world. She devoted her life to the mission of improving the misery and unhealthy living conditions of people all over the world. While she is often known as "the lady with the lamp" for her tireless efforts in the care of the wounded in wartime, Florence Nightingale was also a scientist. She could be understood as the founder of the now popular health care initiative: evidenced-based research, for in 1857 she compiled data and wrote a report of nearly 1,000 pages entitled *Notes Affecting the Health, Efficiency, and Hospital Administration of the British Army*. This report proved conclusively that more men died from the unsanitary conditions of the army hospitals during the war than from bullets on the battlefield. It also showed that the sanitary conditions were so poor in army living quarters that, even in peacetime, the mortality rate of soldiers living in barracks was double that of civilians.

As a person, Nightingale challenged the status quo. As a leader in health care reform, Nightingale used her power and influence, her intellect, her knowledge of statistics, and her persuasive and brilliant personality to affect changes. There was never any question of Nightingale's commitment to making the world a better place.

And what of nursing? What was Nightingale's vision? It is remarkable the extent to which Nightingale set in motion an essential community service, professional nursing, to further human health and well being. Nightingale believed that the nurse's responsibility was to shape the environment, to place the person, ill or well, in the best environment to promote health and healing. She was deeply concerned about unsanitary conditions, and was committed to nurses who provided clean air, clean water and overall sanitary living conditions for their patients. Environmentalists will note that she was ahead of her time in her concern for the benefits of environmental caring and the key role of health professionals in social causes.

While nurses and nursing have embraced many of Nightingale's tenets regarding care of the sick, the profound emphasis that she placed on the social and public health components of nursing are often not as clearly and directly proclaimed. These tenets are most consistent with the basis of philanthropy.

POST NIGHTINGALE VIEWS ON NURSING: AMERICAN NURSING LEADERS

Henderson

Henderson is often referred to as the American Florence Nightingale, for her profound impact on American nursing. She set the stage for many of our health and social developments. You have already been introduced to Henderson's thinking about nursing in the introductory materials for this conference. According to Henderson, the nurse's responsibility is to help people, sick or well, in the performance of those activities contributing to health, its recovery (or to peaceful death), that they would perform unaided if they had the necessary strength, will or knowledge. It is likewise the function of nurses to help people become independent as rapidly as possible.

Peplau

Nursing is a service for people that enhances healing and health by methods that are humanistic....

Orem

Nursing is ... doing for others ... guiding and directing others ... providing physical support ... providing psychological support ... providing a supportive environment ... and teaching.

Rogers

Nursing is creative and imaginative...nurses help individuals, families and groups...achieve maximum well-being....

Other Contemporary Statements
Regarding the Nature of Nursing

Watson

The ethic underlying nursing is humanistic caring...concerned with the human spirit....

King

The focus of nursing is the care of human beings, including health promotion, health maintenance or restoration, care of the sick or injured, and care of the dying...strategies used by nurses include teaching, supporting, counseling, guiding and motivating....

ANA

Nursing is the diagnosis and treatment of human responses to actual and potential health problems....

Donahue

Nursing...the finest art....

Nursing's Code of Ethics

Nursing's code of ethics places responsibility on the nurse to be concerned with the patient's welfare...and to do good, rather than harm. The tenets of nursing's social justice value are imbedded in the code of ethics.

Summary of Values in Professional Nursing

In summary of the nursing perspective...nurses exist as societal agents to help others. Social justice is a value at the very foundation of the profession, a profession characterized by values of courage, commitment to others, caring, humanism, concern for the marginalized, and concern about the human conditions of poverty, illness and suffering.

It is no coincidence that Sigma Theta Tau, the international honor society of nursing, whose 75th anniversary we are celebrating this week at the Biennial Convention, was founded on the values of Love, Courage, Honor, core values within professional nursing. These values are at the roots of our discipline and our professional nursing practice.

THE PHILANTHROPIC VIEW OF THE WORLD

I will now cite exemplars—case studies—of individual philanthropists:

The Legendary Commitment of Congresswoman Frances Payne Bolton to the Profession of Nursing

The roots of Frances Payne Bolton in the Western Reserve of Connecticut (now known as Cleveland) go as deep as the founding of the city. Her great-great-grandfather settled in the area in 1796. Though her background was one of privilege, she had a difficult childhood, and found solace in books and in the solitary pursuit of eastern religions. During her childhood she developed a deep concern for people, especially those less fortunate than herself. She was appalled by poverty and illness, and was first exposed to the dedication of professional nurses in her volunteer activities with the visiting nurses. Her concern for the profession of nursing rose out of these early experiences.

In the early 1920s, while a member of the Nursing Committee of the Lakeside Hospital Board of Trustees, Mrs. Bolton decided that nurses should have the same opportunity as physicians to study at the university. Through her personal dedication to this cause, and her commitment of the initial endowment to begin the School of Nursing at Western Reserve University, Mrs. Bolton began her lifelong involvement with nursing education. In founding the School of Nursing, Mrs. Bolton wrote in her letter to the Western Reserve University president: "...It seems to me of fundamental importance that the School of Nursing should be free in the future to make constructive experiments in the field of nursing education...even though there may be no assurance at the beginning of any particular experiment that the results obtained thereby can be wrought into the permanent policy of the School..."

Later, as a member of the U.S. Congress, she introduced the legendary legislation to fund nursing education at 126 schools of nursing and to support the Cadet Nurse Corps, to prepare the much-needed professional nurses for wartime activities.

Throughout her personal and professional life, Mrs. Bolton lived by the following philosophy: "You must give something to someone to be happier, especially when that gift is your own time and strength." And, importantly, she embodied the philanthropic spirit, so willing to invest her resources, and to take the necessary risks, without any preconceived outcomes.

The Florence Cellar Professorship in Gerontological Nursing, Frances Payne Bolton School of Nursing, Case Western Reserve University, endowed in 1982 with gifts and will commitments totaling more than $1.2M.

Miss Florence Cellar, a graduate of the College of Wooster, enrolled immediately in the Western Reserve University Frances Payne Bolton School of Nursing's new program for college graduates, a generic master's degree program. She received her MN degree in 1938, and for 39 years she developed her professional role in the nursing department at University Hospitals of Cleveland. She was active in all levels of professional organizations including the local association of both ANA and NLN. She also maintained a commitment to the Cellar Lumber Company, established by her father in 1908, serving as board member, president and board chairman.

In funding this professorship, Miss Cellar acknowledged the benefits provided through expert nursing care to her parents in their later years. She stated: "It has been clear to me that we need many more nurses who enjoy working with older people, who understand their needs, and who will keep on seeking better answers for their problems...After watching the excellent care my parents received, I know what monument I wanted to build in their honor, signifying their legacy to all senior citizens...and assisting in preparing future generations of gerontological nurses. This chair is far more appropriate than the tallest column or stone or steel."

The Mellen Foundation

The Mellen Foundation was established by Mr. Edward Mellen in the 1970s to support nursing education in acute and critical care nursing through a national fellowship program.

Mr. Mellen was a self-made millionaire who appreciated the values of hard work and good people. Mr. Mellen's interest in nursing education was developed through his experiences with his wife Louise's care during her many years of living with multiple sclerosis. He knew that it was the quality of nursing care that made a difference in the quality of his wife's daily life. Upon Mr. Mellen's death in 1982, the Mellen Foundation established a professorship in the name of Edward J. and Louise Mellen at the Frances Payne Bolton School of Nursing, Case Western Reserve University, and provided a challenge grant that led to a successful $5M campaign for nursing. The Foundation's decision to target the funds locally rather than nationally following Mr. Mellen's death was based on a long-standing relationship with the Bolton School and Mr. Mellen's belief that he should give back to the community where he made his money.

The Elizabeth Brooks Ford Professorship in Nursing, Frances Payne Bolton School of Nursing, Case Western Reserve University, endowed in 1988 with $1 + M in gifts and commitments.

Mrs. Elizabeth Brooks Ford was an advocate for excellence in the nursing profession. She served as a Red Cross volunteer during World War I, before she married David Knight Ford, a 1921 graduate of Western Reserve University's School of Law, and attorney for Lubrizol Corporation. Mrs. Ford, from a prominent Cleveland family, was not a nurse herself, but she was the founder and first president of the Cleveland Area League for Nursing, the local organization of the National League for Nursing. She served on the board and was president of the Visiting Nurses Association, and was active with the Cleveland Council on Community Nursing. In 1973 she received the Margaret Ireland Award for Community Service from the Women's City Club. Her national service included the U.S. Department of Defense Advisory Committee on Women in the Service.

In endowing the professorship, Mrs. Ford hoped that she would increase the community's awareness and appreciation of the nursing profession.

These are just a few examples of individual philanthropists who contributed to nursing. Other outstanding examples are those of Leonhard and Florentine Fuld in establishing the Helene Fuld Health Trust in honor of their mother and the work and philanthropy of Mary Breckinridge, the founder of the Frontier Nursing Service, a successful social and health care experiment.

Foundation and Corporate Views of Philanthropy

As a form of philanthropy, foundations are established to support specific initiatives. They may be established for a variety of purposes, by groups, families, corporations or individuals. Many foundations are targeted toward giving to causes that advance social justice and the improvement of the health and welfare of people. A glance at the mission and purpose of a few major and minor foundations will provide a capsule view of the consistency with professional nursing's social mandate.

The W.K. Kellogg Foundation (Assets $6B; 1996)

Purpose: Funding priorities include projects designed to improve human well-being through youth, higher education, leadership, community-based and problem-focused health services, food systems, rural life, philanthropy and volunteerism.

The Robert Wood Johnson Foundation (Assets $6B; 1996)

Purpose: To improve the health and health care of Americans. To help the nation and its health care system identify and pursue new opportunities to address persistent health problems and to participate and respond to significant emerging problems. Three basic goals are pursued: 1) To assure that Americans of all ages have access to basic health care. 2) To improve the way services are organized and provided to people with chronic health conditions. 3) To promote health and prevent disease by reducing harm caused by substance abuse. Also seeks opportunities to help the nation address, effectively and fairly, the overarching problem of escalating health care expenditures.

The Josiah Macy Foundation (Assets $130M; 1995)

Purpose: Major interest in medicine and health. Major grant programs are Minorities in Medicine, Medical Education, with emphasis on improving its effectiveness, and training of physicians and other health care professionals; support also for Macy Conferences usually on issues relevant to current program areas. African-Americans; Civil liberties, reproductive rights; health care; economically disadvantaged; Latinos, medical school/education, native Americans; women.

The Hartford Foundation (Assets $384M; 1995)

Fields of interest: community development, education, youth, aged, social services, cultural programs, civic affairs, hospitals, health, AIDS. One of the most striking contemporary foundation gifts to nursing was a 5-year, $5M grant awarded in 1997 to New York University Division of Nursing to create the Hartford Institute for the Advancement of Geriatric Nursing Practice. The foundation invested in this initiative to bring national attention to the care and treatment of older patients, directing multiple audiences to cost-effective strategies for improving the care of the elderly.

The George W. Bock Charitable Trust (Assets $1.2M; 1994)

Fields of interest: child welfare, hospices.

Ann Earle Talcott Fund (Assets $1.8M; 1995)

Fields of interest: social services, family services, disadvantaged, mental health, health services, child welfare, youth, education, literacy, animal welfare.

Community Foundations

Community foundations are almost always geographically confined, but often from one community to another there is great consistency in the mission and goals of these foundations.

The Cleveland Foundation (Assets $903M; 1995)

This pioneer community foundation has served as a model for most community foundations in the U.S.; grants are made to programs serving the greater Cleveland area in the fields of civic and cultural affairs, education and economic development, and health and social services. Current priorities are in economic development; neighborhood development; downtown revitalization; lakefront enhancement; programs dealing with the young, the aged and special constituencies; health care for the medically indigent and for underserved population, and the professional performing and visual arts. Grants are given mainly as seed money for innovative projects or to developing institutions or services addressing unmet needs in the community.

Corporations

While for-profit corporations exist for the purpose of increasing shareholder value, there are many financial and public relations benefits for the commitment of resources to social and health-related philanthropic causes. And often, the dedication of resources to nursing and health projects is just good for business; obviously this is particularly true for the businesses whose products are used by health professionals or directly related to health practices. Two examples of the latter are provided as examples of the corporate fit.

Invacare Corporation

Invacare, an acronym for "innovations in health care," exists worldwide to design, manufacture and distribute the best value in mobility products and medical equipment for people with disabilities and those requiring home health care. Invacare had annual sales in excess of $504M in 1995, serving an estimated $3B global market. The company has experienced 22.5% compound average sales growth per year since 1979. Invacare has supported home care nursing initiatives through continuing education and programmatic support.

Steris Corporation

Steris Corporation, with operating revenues of $7.9M (1994), is a marketer, developer, manufacturer and supplier of sterile processing and infection prevention systems and related consumables and accessories for the worldwide health care market. Steris Corporation has invested in nursing through support of research and development projects and the Association of Operating Room Nurses, and participates in the training of thousands of nurses per year in targeted continuing education programs.

How to Learn About the Resources

Several resources exist to orient the philanthropy student to the foundation and corporation sources of support. These include the Foundation libraries located in Atlanta, Cleveland, New York, San Francisco and Washington; the Foundation Directory which lists foundations by location, and details their purpose and targeted programs, and gives information about assets and recently funded projects; several Foundation Center guides for targeted funding such as that for International and Foreign Programs; and the Directory of Corporate Giving, to name just a few. But this is just step #1.

STEP #2

A Note About Understanding Women as Donors

Sixty percent of the wealth in the U.S. is owned by women. There are several factors about women donors that are relevant to the discussion of the conceptual consistency between philanthropy and professional nursing. Women donors like the collaborative process; they want to know the big picture and at the same time they want the details of a project, and they contribute because they want to make a difference, they want to work toward change. Those of us who are professional nurses would say that these characteristics are common to our profession, perhaps not unrelatedly because we are a female-dominant profession.

STEP #3

The Future: Positioning the Message and the Match

As nurse leaders position themselves in concert with major individual, foundation and corporate philanthropists, they also must position their message in the broader community. It is imperative that the public view nurses as the solution to the health and social challenges of the future. The messengers are all of us, in each and all of our roles. Special messengers include the members of the media, and health care consumers at all levels. Most of all as professional nurses, we must break the silence, and speak about the essence of our work and the care and comfort professional nurses provide for patients. We must be visible in the public forums, at the city clubs, as public speakers regarding health and health care, in the newspapers, on the talk shows, and on the golf courses, in the boardrooms and the benefit circle. In short, as leaders, professional nurses must be active community participants.

SUMMARY

In summary, philanthropy and nursing have as the core the same basic orientation and values. Philanthropy encourages our thinking out of the box; philanthropy seeks solutions to problems, it is action-oriented. It also encourages us to maintain the vision, the spirit, and the commitment to others that is so much a part of who we are and what we do as professional nurses.

For-Profit Public Good

A CONTRADICTION IN TERMS

Robert L. Payton

When President Clinton proposed ambitious expansion of health care services a few year ago we were warned that the result would be "socialized medicine." While we were worrying about that menace, someone overnight—somewhat like the move of the Baltimore Colts to Indianapolis—gave us *capitalized* medicine.

Something very important happened to our society while we were paying attention to other things. If we have in fact moved to a market-driven system of health care it is at least as dramatic a change as any of the radical social movements of recent decades. A for-profit health care system replaces not a system of socialized medicine but a system of *professional* medicine.

That's one focus of these remarks: the rise of *capitalized medicine*. Will the quality of health care improve or decline? Will the trade-offs between cost and service favor cost to such an extent that service deteriorates? Is the quality of health care at risk? Is access to health care at risk?

A second focus of these remarks is not on organizations or institutions or the health care system but on the individuals now called "health care providers." The second issue is *the decline of the professional ideal.*

The third point follows from the first two: If health care provision is to shift from government to marketplace, and if the professional ideal is considered no longer viable, what alternative is there? The third issue is the urgent need for models of *public life based on an ethic of service.*

The competing values involved in the first two issues—the rise of capitalized medicine and the decline of the professional ideal—are those of self-interest and social responsibility. To what extent is health care as a public good a matter of individual responsibility and to what extent is it a matter of social responsibility?

Health care providers presume to care for the health of others. Health care providers make the *professional* claim they are both *competent* and *trustworthy.* The label we attach to those who are considered to be "professionals" in health care creates expectations on the part of our patients and clients, and on society as a whole, that have strong moral obligations. Beyond the expectations held by those immediately involved, there is a larger *social* trust that the *system* of individuals and institutions providing health care services can be trusted to act for the public good.

In the simplest and yet most powerful terms, we of the general public have been encouraged to trust health care professionals to act in our best interest before attending to their own. On balance, we are told, such trustworthiness will serve the larger public good better than any alternative.

That is the professional ideal in health care. The public myth of the physician always on call, never knowingly or intentionally causing harm to his (and increasingly her) patients, is a long-popular theme of our culture. The heroic figure of Florence Nightingale is another widely-held public myth, a model of personal discipline and sacrifice for others. Professional nurses may feel uncomfortable about some aspects of their careers, but more recently Mother Teresa was seen as a model of compassionate care of the kind that characterizes nursing at its best. In much the same way, Albert Schweitzer offered a model that was problematic for some physicians but that personified the ethic of service for most of the general public.

Through the first half of this century, the public myth of the professional ideal prevailed and inspired countless thousands of young people to seek careers as doctors and nurses. Many of us who remember those days from personal experience can refer to people who personified those values in their work. We have actually been cared for by people who seemed to make the myth an honest story and not mere propaganda or sentimental fiction. A friend of mine passed away a few months ago having devoted four decades of professional life to caring for children according to that ideal. My father-in-law, in general practice in a small Iowa river town for fifty years, was a generation older than my friend, but they marched to the same drummer. They put the patient's interest before their own private benefit and convenience. Neither of these men was poor; neither was rich. They cared for their families and they paid their bills.

There was evidence in the lives of those two physicians of the making of a tradition of professionalism, a set of teachings about the practice of medicine and health care based on values that went beyond what the law or profit required. I have been modestly involved as a volunteer with schools of medicine and nursing several times in my career. I know people in those institutions who by personal observation measure up to the ideal of professionalism.

I am not sure the successor generation of physicians and nurses is committed to sustain the professional ideal of health care. The rules of professional practice have changed and professional values may have changed as a result. The word "professional" may no longer mean what it seemed to mean fifty years ago. Some of the changes are clearly for the better—the professions are more open, for example—but some suggest an erosion of central values such as the ethic of service.

Although physicians offer the best known version of the ideal, nurses share in the expectations. As I understand the public view, nurses are thought to be less highly trained than physicians but in their version of the professional ideal nurses are, in special ways, considered better qualified than physicians to deal with many of the most important needs of patients and their families.

As the myth has eroded, physicians now appear to be less concerned with the patient and more concerned with their own well-being; at the same time, public sentiment toward nurses has improved. Nurses are thought to be compassionate as always but also to be more highly trained and competent. The perceived gap of competence between the two professions has narrowed.

The public myth of health care is that physicians and nurses work together, and subordinate their differences for the benefit of the patient. I have also lived long enough to know that such happy cooperation is not always the case. The *ideal*, however, is clear enough: physicians and nurses have an obligation to perform to the best of their ability and to subordinate their self-interest to the best interest of the patient. According to the *ideal*, hospitals are places where patient care is paramount; they have not been thought of, first and foremost, as for-profit business enterprises.

The same expectations of trustworthiness that grew up around physicians and nurses developed in public myths about hospitals. The professional ideal that encourages public trust in physicians and nurses and other health care providers is attributed to the hospitals where they work.

The care and repair of public myth, as one historian describes it, seems increasingly to be shaped in general by the marketplace and its values.

Under socialized medicine, the threat to the public good is that "bureaucrats" will define policy and procedure. The theory of bureaucracy is based on the assumption that the necessary guidelines for performance can be defined by legislation and administrative directive. Socialized medicine thus claims to eliminate favoritism and privilege and to offer the same quality of care to all. Rules and regulations rather than individual judgment determine what is done.

It is customary to scorn bureaucracy and bureaucrats, but we should be reminded of why they came into being in the first place. Prejudice, privilege, favoritism and special interest provided the public demand for the rules and regulations we now disdain.

Capitalized medicine promises something different. The first promise is that competition under capitalized medicine will reduce the cost of health care. The public is receptive to such claims, thanks to the high cost of even routine medical procedures. Skepticism arises from the widely-publicized income of some physicians (nurses are never mentioned). The common morality holds that health care professionals will be comfortable but not rich. A third concern is that hospitals have become notorious not simply for rising costs but for widely-publicized abuses of insured health care programs. For-profit hospitals claim to reduce such costs, but people are skeptical that for-profit hospitals are as committed to quality health care as they are to making a profit. In addition to worrying about physicians and nurses and administrators, the public must now be concerned about the well-being of investors. Not only that: investors are said to have the first claim on assets, and therefore ultimate control of resources.

The marketplace falls short in two ways: on one hand it fails to provide support for the nonmaterial aspects of life, and on the other it seems indifferent to the larger public good in areas like health care and the environment.

If I were mean spirited, I would put it this way: Socialized medicine would make health care into a government bureaucracy, offering low quality at high cost; capitalized medicine would make health care both low-cost and of unreliable quality. Neither socialized medicine nor capitalized medicine would care much about me as a person. I consider that a weakness of those systems, not of me. Sooner or later, systems will be judged by their responsiveness to the complex and changing needs of the individuals they serve.

There is another variation, that of a mixed system of socialized and capitalized medicine, which is what we appear to have. For-profit hospitals compete for government funds to provide health care services to those whom the system of capitalized medicine tends to overlook and for whom socialized medicine seems unable to offer acceptable care. A recent discussion on National Public Radio (why is it that people never seem to shout at each other on National Public Radio?) caused me to think about the version of socialized medicine that is provided by the Veterans Administration. The principal allegation, not denied, was that physicians in Veterans Administration hospitals sometimes fell below acceptable professional standards. That is, the government hospital must compete in the marketplace for medical staff and medical staff are simply not available in sufficient number and quality among people willing to accept lower rates of compensation.

The response of the official on the NPR program was that reform of the Veterans Administration's hospitals and health care services now provides sharply increased compensation to attract better physicians. (Again, nurses are not mentioned.)

Privatizing care for veterans faces stubborn opposition from the veterans' lobby, but veterans are clearly suffering from a decline both in quality and extent of health care as both the expenditure and scope of care are reduced. There appears to be a veteran population that cannot afford the health care it needs, in some cases needs resulting from injuries and disease encountered in the course of military service. The central point of my own reflections is that there is an indispensable element missing from both socialized medicine and capitalized medicine. It is what my assigned title refers to as "the public good." The public good—what we seek in quality and scale, in excellence and access to health care as a system—is not adequately served by a socialized system dependent on regulation, nor is it adequately served by a capitalized system dependent on profit. Neither regulation nor profit, nor some clever combination of those, will provide us with a system of health care that is sufficiently advanced and at the same time sufficiently responsive to the needs of the people it serves.

The missing ingredient is *trust*, social trust in the professional physicians and nurses and trust in the hospitals where they work. Trust cannot be based on the power of government to legislate a health care system that is just and excellent, parsimonious in the use of resources, and generous in its concern for patients and families. Trust cannot be bought by economic performance in the marketplace. Trust can only arise from people who are trustworthy. In this case, that means doctors and nurses who can be trusted in the immediate case to put the best interest of the patient before their own.

Trust in health care as a public good is an urgent issue. That trust has declined sharply in recent decades, both because of the growing inefficiency and lack of responsiveness of government-designed health care programs, and because health care is not merely "a business like any other business." In health care the so-called consumer is at a profound technical disadvantage and psychologically vulnerable as well. The physician's trust in the patient to pay his bills is not equivalent to the patient's trust in the physician's knowledge and skill. The physician can presumably always find another patient if this one dies; the option of finding another physician is not always open to the patient who may suffer terminal disappointment.

Health care problems are enormously complex, so complex and so technical, in fact, that many people simply drop out of the discussion. Yet the *moral* assumptions and actions of health care should be accessible to everyone.

You may find it useful, as I do, to make a distinction between *morals* and *ethics*: morals is about behavior; ethics is about thinking about behavior. That is, we can be moral and not ethical, ethical and not moral. But we become moral—or amoral or immoral—in how we behave; our behavior rather than what we say or even what we think is the best guide to our morality. A man suffered severe burns over fifty percent of his body in the course of rescuing two children from a burning house. He couldn't give reason; it was simply something he had to do. Our behavior defines our morals.

What are the morals of health care? Do we accept some limitations on the health care we receive in order to accommodate the needs of others? Do we as a society make special provision for the weak and poor? Do we entrust the vulnerable to government—to socialized medicine—and expect the strong and affluent to look after themselves? Do we deny medical treatment to those we consider unworthy? Do we deny care to strangers and refugees? Do we admit people to medical treatment only after they have satisfactorily demonstrated their ability to pay for it? Do we permit physicians and nurses to deny their services to people in critical need?

More to the point here: To what extent are life-and-death health care decisions made on financial rather than medical grounds?

I am not asking what *should* be the case; I am asking what actually goes on. What is the common morality of health care in America?

There is a long-established way to think about these problems. I will use the word *professionalism* as a label for it. Professionalism was on its way to becoming a tradition—that is, a set of practices and values sustained over several generations—when it ran into its own failures, largely beginning three decades ago.

Professionalism is an ideal. It first emerged as an ideal in the work of the physician and the nurse. In this country it began to emerge about 150 years ago, as I understand it, when *some* physicians became determined to insist upon a higher standard for *all* physicians than was then generally accepted. Two related criteria were affirmed:

the first was a written code of ethics; the second was inclusion in that pledge of an ethic of service. Physicians were not only expected to adhere to certain standards of trustworthiness in their performance—their *moral* behavior—but to know why they should behave in some ways and not others—their *ethical* understanding.

About fifty years ago, the concept of professionalism was defined by five generally-accepted criteria: (1) competence based on advanced education and training; (2) membership in an association of peers; (3) commitment to a code of ethics; (4) an ethic of service; and (5) autonomy of judgment in practice. The criteria applied not only to physicians but to others in health care. The model attracted those in other fields who wished to identify themselves as adhering to a demanding standard of technical performance *and* personal integrity. Competence as measured by the extent of advanced education and training and specialized expertise lifted some physicians to the highest plane of occupational life in our society. Other participants in providing health care—nurses, especially—insisted that there were other health care values deserving of equal emphasis as well as equal recognition. The discussion was not merely about social status or even income; it also had to do with authority and control. Whatever the substance of the debate, priority was given to the public good of patients and not simply to the private good of health care providers. *Investors* were never mentioned.

Attacks on the professional ideal of the physician began in the 1960s and came largely from the Left of the ideological spectrum. Physicians were alleged to be using their power for their own economic benefit, using advanced training to justify rising incomes. Physicians also extended their control over the content of advanced education as well as admission to medical school and the array of research opportunities. In the jargon of the critics of the Sixties, the medical profession was sexist, racist and generally exclusionist.

Being at the top of the heap, physicians were the first target of the critics, but only the first. More and more occupations claimed the status and privileges associated with the label of professional; "professional" was increasingly equated with "white collar" and little more. Meanwhile, critics increasingly attacked professionalism across the board as self-serving and unjust.

The health care system was accused of being dominated by the American Medical Association, which as the largest and most visible target was in turn accused of being a trade association concerned only about its members' economic advantage rather than a professional association committed to the public good.

The early critics of professionalism tended to support the expansion of government-funded health care to meet the needs of the poor. "One quality of health care for all," they argued, could only be assured by a system grounded in social justice and equal rights. The critique was political more than economic. The measures of success were not efficiency but access, not quality at all costs but equal quality at whatever cost.

In more recent decades the attacks on professionalism have come from the Right and coincided with attacks on government. Health care providers were accused of taking advantage of government-insured programs. They allegedly diverted resources that were intended to help patients to use them instead to ease their own lives and fatten their own incomes. Because government-funded programs underwrote costs, the cost-cutting disciplines of the marketplace were missing. The sins of government-supported health care were alleged to be incompetence, intrusiveness, inefficiency and corruption.

In this critique, health care providers who work for the government are expected to maintain the same standards that would be expected of them in private professional situations. It is a sobering reminder that in many societies in which health care is wholly government-provided, health care *professionals* as such don't exist; health care *bureaucrats* do. Non-medical bureaucrats often make medical decisions and "professional" considerations are set aside or overruled.

The positive case from the Right praises the merits of competition. For-profit health care advocates claim that a well-managed clinic or hospital will show a profit—there will be enough patients to pay for the medical care they need and want and can afford. Physicians and nurses will share in the financial benefits depending on their contribution to the financial bottom-line. The competition for the patient as consumer will cause health care providers and their institutions to provide a steadily higher level of quality care.

Or such is the new public myth of for-profit health care as we are urged to accept it.

The language of health care has shifted from the language of professionalism and the public good to the language and values of the private marketplace. If health care is an economic activity first and foremost, then its economic self-interest must be served.

The values of the marketplace tend to be reduced to performance as measured by short-term financial results. For the layperson, the most telling argument against for-profit health care is that medical decisions will not rely on the autonomous judgments of physicians and nurses but on non-medical administrators or on medical personnel functioning as non-medical administrators. Those decision-making processes provide the media's horror-stories that have the general public in a state of anxiety.

Neither socialized medicine nor capitalized medicine offer the promise of a health care system that is optimally excellent and accessible. Each one promises more than it can deliver.

Only the tradition of professionalism seems to get to the core of the problem: an ethical system based on *private* responsibility for the *public* good.

The trust that is given by—or exacted from—the patient relies on a high degree of trustworthiness. The health care provider accepts a responsibility commensurate with higher status and sometimes a higher quality of life. For the health care provider, at least as I have known them, *self-respect* is an important governor. Self-respect, as people are eager to point out, is more important than self-esteem. Some professionals will find self-esteem in affluence; but in my opinion the true professional can find self-respect only in an ethic of service.

We have all known cultures of health care in which professional values permeate everything that goes on. But my sense is that such places are diminishing in number; that professionals themselves are diminishing in number and in influence. The professional ideal is at risk.

Health care is a public good, at least in aspiration. Societies seem always to fall short of making a high quality of care accessible to all. In our search for the best answer we turned to government provision and control. When that proved to be inadequate, we turned to the private marketplace. There seem to be deficiencies in that system, too, especially in providing health care for the poor and most vulnerable, but even in the norms of care for patients able to pay.

The third approach discussed here is the professional ideal: Health care is guided by physicians and nurses and their best judgment of what health care should provide and for whom. The professional ideal has fallen victim of its own weaknesses, attacked with stunning effect from both Left and Right. The stewards of the professional ideal—the professionals themselves—seem to have lost their sense of mission.

Two concluding thoughts occur to me. The first is to ask about the sources of social trust and how those sources might be replenished and renewed. There is no public good without social trust. A society like ours with an extensive reliance on voluntary action for the public good is likely to be a society with a large capacity for social trust.

The second thought is that we always need *models of public life*. The professional health care provider was such a model. The scientist has been another. The politician as public servant was another. These career models are held up to young people as models of public life because they are expected to serve the public good and not simply their own *private* good. We do not ask that of business people or ordinary citizens—we can confine ourselves to our private lives and measure success by our private benefits. The argument here is that the concern with private benefit, whatever the great achievements of private enterprise, fails in important ways to serve the public good. *Some* among us must devote their lives to the public good. *Some* among us must serve as models of trustworthiness.

Philanthropy may provide some answers. Philanthropic giving may provide the marginal subsidy that makes the professional ideal sustainable over time. Philanthropy can support initiatives like the new center on health care ethics and professionalism that I've become associated with. Philanthropy can support conferences like this one, bringing health care professionals together in candid self-assessment.

Philanthropy can subsidize the education and training of young people drawn to the professional ideal as their model of public life. Philanthropy can support physicians and nurses whose values add a moral dimension to rules and regulations and to cost-benefit analysis. Philanthropy can subsidize professionals who wish to devote part of their time and energy to community service, like those in the so-called CATCH program of the American Academy of Pediatrics. Philanthropy can fund sabbaticals for physicians and nurses to advance their social knowledge and ethical understanding as well as their technical competence.

If we think of philanthropic giving and service as working at the margin to make health care better, rather than as a means of providing the economic and technological infrastructure, philanthropy should bring the moral and ethical voice to the discussion of health care.

"Voluntary action for the public good" links philanthropy to concepts like professionalism. It is in fact the *philanthropic* value of concern for the well-being of others that lifts professionals above their peers in the private marketplace. Philanthropy and professionalism, among other instruments of the public good, rest most fundamentally on moral rather than on economic or political values.

Like all ideals, philanthropy and professionalism are models of public life that fall short of the ideal in practice. Vice as well as virtue is evident in all human affairs, including the most noble. But if our models of public life, both individual and institutional, do not contain a strong moral discipline, we lose the framework that creates social trust. That's what the struggle is about.

7

Voice Vs. Loyalty
THE DILEMMA OF NURSES

Angela Barron McBride

In 1970, Hirschman's classic, *Exit, Voice, and Loyalty* (subtitled *Responses to Decline in Firms, Organizations, and States*), was published. In it, he boiled down the strategies available to members of organizations in decline to: exit (leaving the organization) and voice (speaking up critically for the purpose of positive change). While he eschewed the notion that some optimal mix of exit or voice could be prescribed, he did point out "the hidden potential of whatever reaction mode is currently neglected" (p. 126). And it is with this in mind that I wish to consider a major dilemma of nursing in this period of rapid change in healthcare organizations, the fact that professional nurses are so often torn between voice and loyalty, and to explore the hidden potential of nurses speaking up more at this time when our caregiving systems appear to be, if not in decline, at least under severe assault.

Though nurses are professionals who are presumed by the public to wield power by virtue of their numbers and knowledge base, their authority (particularly in relationship to medicine) has been sufficiently unsupported, so that they frequently are in the situation of having responsibility without corresponding authority and voice at the organizational table. This situation has implications for philanthropy, which is committed, as one of its primary objectives, to empowering the not-for-profit sector in those worthwhile areas where it has traditionally had little or no voice. Nursing and philanthropy also share common ground in their concerns about asking the public for support—nursing has not consistently made clear to the public what it is asking for, whereas philanthropy can inform these matters by reminding us that the "receive" part of "ask and ye shall receive" is contingent on the "ask" part. It is accordingly my belief that one important interface between nursing and philanthropy must be nursing's learning from philanthropy how to make the case statement for needed resources more clearly and forcefully than in the past, a process whereby nursing is likely to become re-energized as it voices important health values.

VOICE VS. LOYALTY

Because the overwhelming majority of nurses work for institutions, as opposed to being professionals who "have their own practices" (the preferred mode of operations for medicine, dentistry and law), they operate as employees in service to agencies rather than as freewheeling entrepreneurs. Historically, this has meant that nurses have been less likely to dissent as individuals, and more likely to speak only as part of the Department of Nursing Services. They collectively shape institutional protocols and policies, and are expected to act in terms of them. Because they have 24-hour institutional responsibility for patients' activities of daily living and functional abilities, their work does not lend itself to neat segmentation in terms of ward rounds, office visits, or 50-minute therapy sessions. Such a non-segmented purview requires nurses to work collectively around the clock within complicated systems, but it also has a chilling effect on voicing concerns or criticisms, for such behavior is easily construed as disloyal to the group effort. Moreover, it is always difficult to get a large group to speak with one voice, which further limits nursing's point of view to those general statements likely to survive repeated committee debate.

Because most nurses work as part of a collaborative team, their individual contributions are likely to be invisible. For example, a magazine account of care of the homeless may name the physician working on the project, but label a photograph of the physician surrounded by two nurses as "Dr. John Smith with his nurses," when the latter are literally providing 90% of the care being delivered as part of a particular initiative. If individuals are un-named, then so are their contributions. In the last decade or two, complicated organ transplants have been likely to garner media attention for their high-tech procedures, but not the extensive nursing care subsequently required by such patients. I had personal experience with this phenomenon when Yale went co-ed at the undergraduate level. A booklet entitled *She* was developed at the time which listed all resources available to women and the names of all female faculty. However, only the dean's name was listed under "School of Nursing." For a complete listing of that faculty, one was supposed to apply to the dean's office. Since that booklet was used extensively during the transition period as a resource for appointing women as "fellows" within the residential colleges and for other similar integration purposes, the nursing faculty were reduced to a collective presence and thereby rendered invisible in the process. The implication was "if you've seen one nurse, you've seen them all," yet no one comparably expects that members of English, Sociology, and Physics Departments are all the same.

The integrative nature of nursing is difficult to convey, and descriptions of the field can make it seem mundane—health education, emotional support and palliative care do not look particularly flashy. Nursing is much more than a series of discrete tasks performed, yet it is the tasks that capture attention, and they may be dismissed as repetitive rather than important. The nurse may be performing a relatively menial task, such as a dressing change, and also be conducting a mental status examination, checking for drug side-effects, and preparing the patient for discharge, but only the wound care may be obvious to an onlooker. The patient may describe a nurse as personable because she stops by to ask how he is feeling, but surveillance and assessment are the key features of the exchange from the nurse's perspective, not cheerful personality (Gordon, 1997).

To the extent that nursing has been largely peopled by women, "voice vs. loyalty" has been a special problem for the field. Because women have historically enjoyed less geographic mobility than their male counterparts, they have felt constrained to choke down any criticism of their workplace because exit is less of an option when choice of where to work is severely limited. Since the doctor-nurse relationship has historically been regarded as not unlike the husband-wife relationship, the female nurse was expected to influence through indirect means rather than authority-based statements of opinion (Stein, 1967)—"Doctor Jones, don't you think we should do_____for Mr. Smith?" When language is indirect, however, the person seems vague and unfocused when that may be far from the case.

The traditional situation of nursing should be of mounting concern to physicians at this point in time, because their own practice is being shaped by institutional pressures as they increasingly function as salaried workers within large integrated networks. Physicians are expressing growing concern that such organization of their practice will "ruin their professionalism" (Kane, 1994, p. 6) and that they "are becoming just technicians" (Montague, 1995, p. 56). The constraints of such a situation were particularly obvious in one restructured institution's definition of collaboration as "staff, physicians and the leadership working together," for that conceptualization of values made nurses mere staff, but it also separated physicians from the leadership.

Voice and Professionalism

There is nothing inherently wrong in nurses being part of a hospital staff, nor in all physicians not being presumed automatically to be organizational leaders, nor in leadership that is not peopled only by physicians. What is problematic is when nurses are regarded only as providing "coverage" rather than as empowered professionals, or clinicians (nurses, physicians and their other colleagues) are not given voice in the leadership of a health care organization. With burgeoning concern that health care be cost effective, there has been a tendency to elevate those with business backgrounds to top leadership positions with a corresponding erosion in caregivers' practice, particularly of those professional responsibilities that are costly while not providing immediate benefit to either the patient or to the institution's bottom line, for example, shared decision making; the allocation of professional time to non-patient care activities; a commitment to lifelong professional learning; and various extensions of the body of knowledge (Wennberg, 1994).

The word "profession" has been linked to "voice" for centuries, since it derives from the Latin *profitere*, which means "'to promise publicly' that you will do something" (Curtin, 1996c, p. 72). What professionals traditionally promised was to be patients' advocates (Curtin, 1996a), but that clarity of focus has been eroded by a growing belief that health care providers must also become responsible stewards of society's resources (Williams, 1992). In this view, health care providers have an overarching responsibility to husband resources for the good of the many, perhaps even more than they have a duty to do right for the individual patient. Such an economic emphasis raises questions about the many services that are not obviously profitable from indigent care to subsidizing the education of health care professionals and their research (Curtin, 1996b).

Indeed, it is the act of profession—what Pellegrino (1995) sees as the covenant of trust established in the healing relationship—that may be most under attack in today's world, because health care increasingly seems to be obsessed with reducing care to a set series of reimbursable procedures and strictly enforced time guidelines. Being a health care professional is more than a selling of services in the marketplace. The health care professions share with philanthropy a fundamental commitment to the common public good. Even though professionals have a right to earn a decent living commensurate with education and experience, they are not expected to take advantage of their patients' vulnerability nor the accompanying knowledge imbalance. Moreover, professional exchanges are expected to be "transformational, rather than merely transactional" (May, 1992, p. 38), in that they are not only expected to dispense technical services but professionals are expected to teach their patients how to avoid similar problems in the future (Benner, 1997)—similar to the distinctions made between charity (distributing food to the hungry) and philanthropy (teaching the hungry how to fish). The transformational, alas, may take longer that the tranactional, and is impossible to calibrate with precision in business terms!

Nursing—A Clear Voice

Nursing has been concerned about whether it meets the criteria for being considered a profession since I was a student almost 40 years ago. The characteristics a profession was supposed to meet included: development of a body of scientific knowledge; use of the scientific method to enlarge the body of knowledge; education within institutions of higher education (as opposed to an apprenticeship system); control of professional policy and activity; subscription to a code of ethics; lifetime commitment; and service to the public (Keogh, 1997). That is roughly the order in which these criteria have long been discussed, with service to the public not typically mentioned first, because it has long been presumed to be a given.

During my tenure in the profession, the field has been necessarily more concerned with proving that it has a body of specialized knowledge than that it exists to serve the public, because its stereotyped image emphasized handmaiden service more than it described nurses as expert authorities. A la Nightingale, the various definitions of nursing described the nurse as putting patients in the best condition for nature to act upon them—"helping people (sick or well) in the performance of those activities contributing to health, or its recovery (or to a peaceful death) that they would perform unaided if they had the necessary strength, will or knowledge" (Henderson, 1978, p. 34). Such definitions seemingly emphasized common sense, but what most people forgot in that sense is not common. It takes considerable education and experience to be capable of such seamless practice. Such definitions also seemed to equate nursing with personal care, and thereby downplayed all that nurses do to facilitate care given by others, design programs to meet the needs of vulnerable populations, and develop caregiving systems that permit personal care to be realized. Indeed, one of the thorny continuing issues in nursing is that those not involved in delivering personal care are too often dismissed as not "real" nurses, which has had the effect of dismissing all researchers, educators and administrators as not "real" nurses thus stilling their voices to a significant extent.

Is nursing capable of a clear voice? Yes. With the establishment of the National Institute for Nursing Research within the National Institutes of Health, nursing science has gained respectability and visibility (McBride, 1987). At the time that President Clinton mounted his push for health care reform, nursing developed an agenda that was generally endorsed by the field (Moss, 1995). With the development of differentiated practice by level of academic preparation, agreed-upon competencies exist. For example, the Indiana Organization of Nurse Executives and the Indiana nursing deans/directors have recently agreed on the competencies graduates of associate-degree programs, bachelor's-level programs, and master's programs should have two years after graduation. This clarity means that educators can now orient new students to those expectations from the start; competencies to be developed can be identified in every course; graduates can refer to that listing of competencies to describe themselves in job interviews; and prospective employers can have a better sense of what to expect from new workers.

If nursing can have a clear voice, then what would it say? Because nursing is concerned less with disease per se and more with dis-eases (actual or potential threats to well-being and quality of life), it has the potential of speaking out on some of the matters that most trouble the public, the lifestyle issues that lead to disease over time—poor hygiene, smoking, unsafe sex, lack of exercise, substance abuse, faulty nutrition, lack of stress management, accidents, dangerous environments, and other risk-taking behaviors. Alas, nursing tends to be judged in its practice more in terms of its capabilities of providing physician-substitute services than in terms of its expertise in the aforementioned areas (Safriet, 1992).

The promise to do something to alleviate dis-ease, which is core to the nursing profession, has not changed. The task of nursing (and of philanthropy, too) remains the improvement of the lives of individuals. But as Curtin (1996c, p. 72) cautions us:

> What has changed is the type of disease (chronic versus acute) that afflicts most people in post- industrialized countries; the effectiveness of various therapies in treating specific problems; the sophistication of our knowledge (relating disease state and lifestyle choices, understanding that symptom control and cure are not necessarily related, identifying multiple variables and their inter- relationships); and the costs generated by "success."

For Curtin, it is important that we revitalize "old" professional commitments, but do so aware of the need for "new" knowledge of lifestyle choices/personal responsibility, possible outcomes and the limits of success. That is a formidable task for nursing, and one that requires collaborative practice with Medicine and a link with philanthropy to be fully achieved.

RESOURCE DEVELOPMENT

Nurses have long been associated with not-for-profit agencies, where "doing good" was too often believed to be rationale enough for being supported professionally. Indeed, nursing students continue to lament that "the general public is not yet aware of the expertise, knowledge and skills of nurses today" (Rowentree, Wells & Sterzing, 1995). We nurses, if anything, have tended to have a self-righteous streak, whereby others are regularly taken to task for not understanding us and our value to the larger society. Most of us have been educated to assess thoroughly all of our patients' needs and try to meet them, leaving us feeling frequently ineffective and depressed because that is mission impossible, all the more so in today's environment of limited hospital stays and limited reimbursement for services.

Make no mistake, there is a problem in how the public sees nursing. For example, the latest round of the Women's Movement was much more effective in encouraging women to enter fields previously dominated by men than in changing stereotyped thinking about the fields traditionally peopled by women. Moreover, medicine is frequently used as a generic term to subsume all of health care, much the way "he" was used generically to include "she," with the same invisibility resulting for nursing as was true for women in that pronoun debate. Despite those deep-seated problems, however, nurses must do a better job of articulating how they meet public need, rather than getting angry that that is the case. To return to an earlier point, the time is ripe for nursing's service to the public to be reaffirmed before any statement of scientific integrity, because the former is necessary even to obtain needed resources for the latter.

The current health care situation, with its emphasis on managed care, pits cost and efficiency against accepted practices and clinical standards. Quality, access and cost-effectiveness are purportedly the holy triumvirate, but market considerations have seemingly shaped practice more than the other considerations. We all know some horror stories where corporate greed resulted in health care abuse (Mohr, 1997). The enormity of the changes taking place with the advent of more for-profit care and not-for-profit institutions being increasingly concerned about their financial well-being has left health care professionals worried about client outcomes and competitive survival (Ebrat & Hollerman, 1996). Yet such massive change also offers the possibility of new opportunities in several areas: Physicians and nurses are experiencing comparable changes, so new opportunities for collaboration exist. Limited resources mean that all health care professionals have to readjust their role responsibilities to include resource development as part of their leadership skills. Such resource development will, in turn, force health care professionals to become clearer about their mission, goals and anticipated outcomes as they set forth their case statements for philanthropic support. Finally, not-for-profit institutions will be forced to elaborate on how any savings are reinvested in longer-term benefits.

The more physicians get away from rugged individualism as their principal way of operating, which they will as their practice becomes embedded in large integrated networks, the more they will be constrained by some of the same forces that have long affected nurses. Both fields are being challenged to increase their productivity and are threatened by "downward substitution" pressures, which hopefully offers the promise that the fields could work together to shape a new kind of collaboration, for example, one that uses nurses creatively to keep vulnerable populations out of expensive acute-care settings and to manage chronic conditions. But such a collaboration must be predicated on respect for what each field contributes without either physicians being obsessed with the requirement that nurses always work "under" them or nurses representing themselves as mini-physicians. The new structures taking shape offer the possibility that the relationship between these two major fields might be better defined. For example, the consolidation of Methodist Hospital of Indianapolis, Riley Children's Hospital and University Hospital into Clarian Health Partners has resulted in a committee structure that brings nursing and medicine to the table in new ways around education and research.

Both fields are being similarly affected by financial pressures, and have to consider new funding strategies for their institutions to prosper. Funding for non-profit organizations is going to come increasingly from:

- more efficient delivery of services
- more mergers, acquisitions, partnerships and joint ventures
- more emphasis on gifts as investments, rather than as contributions
- more entrepreneurial activity
- more reliance on fee-for-service income
- more creative finance, such as finding paying uses for property assets
- more productivity out of the fundraising department

(Lenkowsky, 1996, p. 8)

As a result, both fields will have to socialize their students to develop such skills through new partnerships with philanthropy, which in turn will require both fields to do a better job of articulating what they are doing in ways that garner public support. With merger mania, it is particularly important that fundraising stay community based, because donors are more inclined to invest where they obtain their services and have a history (Pallarito, 1995), so health care professionals will have to learn to tell the story of what they are doing locally even more effectively.

In no area do medicine and nursing have more in common than in their shared concern for ensuring that their practices are not limited by the for-profit obsession with short-term benefits over long-term considerations. What is commercial—corporate profit-taking, risk avoidance, gag rules, skimming off of profitable services—can be antithetical to community responsibility and over-time quality health care (McArthur & Moore, 1997). This is particularly the case in academic health centers whose mission includes teaching and research in addition to the provision of health care. The benefits that accrue from these activities are not likely to be immediate, thus requiring long-term investment that is not appealing to for-profit organizations. A case in point is the research that was reported in the August 27th issue of the *Journal of the*

American Medical Association in which long-term benefits of home visitation by nurses on maternal life course, childhood injuries and child abuse/neglect were found fifteen years later (Kitzman et al., 1997; Olds et al., 1997). Nurses and physicians, joined by their business colleagues, should collaborate also in devising new definitions of what it means to be a not-for-profit organization—one where the dividends resulting from cost-effective care are returned to the public stakeholders to support teaching and research.

CONCLUSION

Let me end by summarizing my belief in the importance of the link between nursing (and medicine) and philanthropy at this point in time. Nursing and philanthropy share many values—a commitment to address the root cause(s) of suffering; advocacy for those unable to speak on their own behalf; dedication to action for the public good; an appreciation of the education needed to achieve self-help; an appreciation of the importance of voluntary association to give voice to matters that cannot be easily raised by the vulnerable and the disenfranchised; the need for sound stewardship of limited resources; an interest in the successful administration of not-for-profit organizations; and a dedication to limiting mortality, compressing morbidity and maximizing quality of life. If they can work together—nursing learning from philanthropy how to become more adroit at making its case for the purpose of obtaining public support; philanthropy learning from nursing how to link voluntary effort to promote human welfare with professional effort to promote human welfare—both fields are likely to gain substantially.

Block, in his 1993 book on the subject, suggests that *stewardship* is an alternative to traditional hierarchical notions of care taking, for the concept eschews ownership of problems and organizations for a more liberating sense of shared, broad based partnership. It may be that nurses and philanthropists are being called to implement such notions of stewardship in creating a new healthcare future.

References

Benner, P. (1997). A dialogue between virtue ethics and care ethics. **Theoretical Medicine,** 18(1-2), 47-61.

Block, P. (1993). Stewardship. San Francisco: Berrett-Koehler.

Curtin, L. L. (1996a). The ethics of managed care—Part 1: Proposing a new ethos? **Nursing Management, 27,** 18-19.

Curtin, L.L. (1996b). The ethics of managed care—Part 2: Diagnosis: The world as it is ... Nursing Management, 27, 53-55.

Curtin, L. L. (1996c). The ethics of managed care—Part 3: Toward a common vision. Nursing Management, 27, 71-74.

Ebrat, K.S. & Hollerman, C.E. (1996). The leadership dance. **Journal of Nursing Administration,** 26(4), 13-15.

Gordon, S. (1997). Life support. Three nurses on the front lines. Boston: Little, Brown.

Henderson, V. (1978). Practice of and preparation for nursing. In V. Henderson & G. Nite (Eds.), **Principles and practice of nursing** (pp. 3-119), 6th ed. New York: Macmillan.

Hirschman, A.O. (1970). **Exit, voice, and loyalty. Responses to decline in firms, organizations, and states.** Cambridge, MA: Harvard University Press.

Kane, W.J. (November 5, 1994). Face to face. Should integrated networks employ physicians? **Hospitals & Health Networks.**

Keogh, J. (1997). Professionalization of nursing: Development, difficulties and solutions. **Journal of Advanced Nursing, 25,** 302-308.

Kitzman, H., Olds, D.L., Henderson, Jr., C.R., Hanks, C., Cole, R., Tatelbaum, R, McConnochie, K.M., Sidora, K., Luckey, D. W., Shaver, D., Engelhardt, K., James, D., & Barnard, K. (1997). Effect of prenatal and infancy home visitation by nurses on pregnancy outcomes, childhood injuries, and repeated childbearing. A randomized controlled trial. **Journal of the American Medical Association, 278,** 644-652.

Lenkowsky, L. (1996). **The "Contract with America": An opportunity for philanthropy.** Indianapolis: Indiana University Center on Philanthropy.

May, W.F. (1992). The beleaguered rulers: The public obligation of the professional. **Kennedy Institute of Ethics Journal, 2,** 25-41.

McArthur, J. H., & Moore, F.D. (1997). The two cultures and the health care revolution: Commerce and professionalism in medical care. **Journal of the American Medical Association, 277,** 985-989.

McBride, A.B. (1987). The National Center for Nursing Research. **Social Policy Report** (a publication of the Society for Research in Child Development), 2(2), 1-11.

Mohr, W.K. (1997). Outcomes of corporate greed. **Image: Journal of Nursing Scholarship.** 29, 39-45.

Montague, J. (April 5, 1995). Managing. Eroding empires. **Hospitals & Health Networks,** 56-58.

Moss, M.T. (1995). Principles, values, and ethics set the stage for managed care nursing. **Nursing Economics, 13,** 276-284, 294.

Olds, D.L., Eckenrode, J., Henderson, Jr., C.R., Kitzman, H., Powers, J., Cole, R., Sidora, K., Morris, P., Pettitt, L.M., & Luckey, D. (1997). Long-term effects of home visitation on maternal life course and child abuse and neglect. Fifteen-year follow-up of a randomized trial. **Journal of the American Medical Association, 278,** 637-643.

Pallarito, K. (October 2, 1995). Healthcare philanthropy's big challenge. **Modern Healthcare,** 76-86.

Pellegrino, E.D. (1995). Toward a virtue-based normative ethics for the health professions. **Kennedy Institute of Ethics Journal, 5,** 253-277.

Rowntree, J. A., Well, L.M., & Sterzing, M.M. (1995). The emergence of nursing as a profession. **NSNA/Imprint,** 42(2), 30, 39.

Safriet, B.J. (1992). Health care dollars and regulatory sense: The role of advanced practice nursing. **Yale Journal on Regulation,** 9, 417-488.

Wennberg, J.E. (1994). Health care reform and professionalism. **Inquiry,** 31, 296-302.

Williams, A. (1992). Cost-effectiveness analysis: Is it ethical? **Journal of Medical Ethics,** 18, 7-11.

Nursing and Philanthropy
A METAPHOR FOR THE TWENTY-FIRST CENTURY

Warren F. Ilchma

"Nursing and philanthropy" may constitute at first glance a curious conjunction. Philanthropy is a gift; nursing is a service for which compensation is expected. An expanded view of both, however, makes the conjunction sensible. Philanthropy is often defined as voluntary giving, voluntary serving and voluntary association with a view towards some vision of the public good. Philanthropy is concerned with the welfare of unknown others, welfare beyond the family. While nursing cannot be characterized as "voluntary" in the most literal sense, I would argue that as a profession nursing is a calling that is predicated on ethical principles, not profit or power, and that the whole array of activities on behalf of the various publics nursing serves may be considered as a variation on the notion of philanthropy.

Making this conjunction sensible is important to me because the separation of values from higher education and especially the education of professionals has resulted in an inadequate preparation for the leadership we expect from the educated. This is why philanthropic studies as an interdisciplinary perspective was developed in the first place: to regain a place in the curriculum and in practice for an understanding of the highest values of community, that saw in voluntary action for the public good a key to understanding what defines a good society and the good life, both here and everywhere. By emphasizing in a nurse's education the civic roles, informed by philanthropy, that they have played and will play, we may compensate for the teachings of the social sciences that predicate motivation on immediate self-interest; we may compensate for the humanities and their preoccupation with power of one sort or the other or their dealing with values as if they were language games; and we may compensate for the teaching within professional programs that mix imparting skill with seeking to advance the interest of one profession at the expense of other professions. In every sense, I believe that bringing the notion of philanthropic roles into the education of nurses expands their vision and equips them for stronger leadership responsibilities and to become better people. It also enriches our understanding of philanthropy.

There are four philanthropic roles I believe nurses play. The first is as a participant in the maintaining and improving of civil society. The second is as a mentor to new generations of nurses. The third role is as the chief point in health care where volunteers are assisted in playing their roles in voluntary serving, where their competence is enriched and their motivation sustained. Fourth, nurses play direct philanthropic roles, either as fundseekers for their institutions or as philanthropists, giftgivers themselves in their own right to causes that they value. Of great importance, too, these roles are more often than not played in settings that are nonprofit and philanthropic in character. Surely, that fact alone warrants some attention in the preparation of nurses. My contention is that these philanthropic roles are not prepared for and therefore they are less well performed than might otherwise be the case.

Why should understanding these roles—and hence playing them better—be important? Health—construed most broadly—is a major area of value for public debate. The debate takes place in many forums— governmental and non-governmental, professional and general. Health is a major agenda for civil society, as well as for the state. Indeed, it serves as a metaphor for what we are collectively seeking. What is said to maintain or improve health ultimately consumes a very high proportion of our Gross Domestic Product, as well as our personal income and public revenues, and we pay considerable attention to the subject in public and private forums. To insure well-modulated voices from one of the most knowledgeable sectors of the community on this subject—understanding what they bring to the discussion—is mandatory. In addition, the civic skills nurses acquire in the course of their education and work—skills of negotiations, seeing problems holistically, conferring trust through teamwork, and encouraging discussion of common ends—are skills always in short supply for society as a whole. Second, if a key dimension of effectiveness is what we learn beyond the classroom from more experienced others, then explicit recognition of the obligation of nurses to mentor, to voluntarily give their knowledge, as well as seeking systematically ways to improve the process, will rebound to the advantage of both individuals and society. Third, volunteers constitute a workforce in health care that is 16% of the total workforce—almost 1 in 5. They are indispensable to achieving an organization's mission, whomever it serves and whatever it does. They are more often than not in the stewardship of nurses. To allow the energy and commitment of volunteers in health care to be wasted is a moral issue as well as a practical one. Nurses must be alert to their position in this relationship. Fourth, in terms of revenue, sixty-six percent of health care takes place in nonprofit settings, philanthropic institutions run by unpaid boards of trustees. Failure to understand the peculiarities of that form—particularly the concern over private inurement, the conditions of professional trust, and the prominence of the use of volunteers—may spell the difference between satisfaction and dissatisfaction in one's work, between good performance and ordinary performance. Understanding that mode of organization also reminds us of what we may lose as the ways of the market become more acceptable in health care. Finally, although private and foundation giving represent less than four percent of revenue in health care, the sums from these sources often represent the defining difference in most institutions, the source of real improvement and change. For nurses to see themselves as partners in an institution's philanthropic fundraising and as givers themselves to things they value is conducive to how they are valued and how they value themselves.

What in the experience of nurses makes me believe that they are likely to play these philanthropic roles with unusual insight? First, nurses have taken on an obligation to serve unknown others, the furthest Mysian as the Stoics called them, the strangers in our midst who have claim on our common decency. This obligation is often used as one definition of acting philanthropically. Second, throughout the long history of nursing there has been a commitment to understanding health in a holistic way, to look for the root causes of suffering and to try to address them as well as to treat the immediate, an illness versus a disease model, if you will, with nurses opting for the former. Seeking root causes and systemic explanations, and trying to address them, is another dimension associated with philanthropy. Third, a nurse is deeply aware of the ensemble of skills necessary for any task, how interdependence and cooperation are superior to competition and autonomy in many settings. Finally, there is the exercise of these various orientations in a public realm. Nursing is not a private action; it always takes place in a public arena. By what they say and do, not only with those under their care but also as citizens, nurses are, in fact, public teachers.

Whether these philanthropic roles are the most important roles nurses play, I cannot say. They are, however, relatively unrecognized in formal instruction or in professional rhetoric. Playing them well is important to society as a whole but also to the leadership nurses hope to exercise in the health care community. I would also argue that some of these roles were more explicitly played in the past and that they have been obscured by other values—among them, the long drive for professional status, embodied in university education and parity with the medical profession and the working out of the complications of gender, class and race. It might well be that this is a propitious time to consider philanthropy as an energizing theme for nursing in the period ahead. And for nursing to be a subject matter that advances all of philanthropic studies.

Let me deal with several of these points in greater detail.

CIVIL SOCIETY

The notion of civil society has become quite faddish these days, but the idea is more than a fad. It has a long lineage into the religious wars of the 17th century and later in the rise of independent commerce in the late 18th century. It has acquired currency in this era by those wishing to overcome totalitarianism in Eastern Europe and the former Soviet Union and by those in Western Europe and America seeking to rebuild a sense of community in a context of declining confidence in government and the divisions arising from economic dislocation, racial diversity and income inequality. What the notion has consistently meant has been there should be a sphere apart from the state where individuals can realize their values, that this sphere is characterized by visions of a public good, and through participation in it one contributes to that vision and becomes in a larger sense a real "citizen." Civil society is beyond the state, independent of the state, and a source of changing the agenda and the conduct of the state. From civil society comes the agenda for public change. It is thought to be related to philanthropy because it is predicated on voluntary association for the achievement of some public value.

Let me indulge in what the eminent historian William McNeill calls mythistory, our reconstruction of the past in light of contemporary needs and values, a transcending of the purely factual nature of our symbols from the past, to portray what we value in the present. In an exercise of mythistory, I would like to say that nurses in the past had a better sense of their public roles and these were large roles. In the chief issues that engaged the American polity since the civil war—post-slavery reconstruction, temperance, nutrition, public health, population planning, safe working conditions, child labor prohibitions, maternal and child health, physical and vocational education, building standards, voting, civil rights and integration, gender equity, environment, etc., etc.,—issues that were discussed in myriad forums before they ever entered the realm of politics and the state, there was leadership in all of them from nurses. Symbolically, Florence Nightingale would be my starting point, a starting point of quintessential civil society dimensions—service, trust, considering problems holistically, the need for public representation of what one valued. My mythistory for the United States would begin with the Sanitary Commissions of the Civil War; dwell on the work of Clara Barton, Lavinia Dock, Lillian Wald, Margaret Sanger, Annie W. Goodrich; and end with the present leadership of feminist organizations and the presidency of the fifth largest private foundation (Rebecca Rimel) to illustrate that the chief issues engaged by civil society and eventually the state had prominent leadership from the nursing community.

The mythistory would view the founding and present functions of organizations like Sigma Theta Tau or the former National Association of Colored Graduate Nurses as efforts to prepare nurses for their responsibilities in civil society. The requirements in student chapters to discuss issues beyond the profession; to acquire habits of problem identification, deliberation, action and implementation; and to develop strategies for presenting views to a larger public all prepared nurses for leadership in professional associations, service clubs, churches, and, for some, eventually the state. In essence they were training academies for civil society and would be stronger in that role today if they were so recognized.

MENTORING AND VOLUNTEERS

It may be trite to say that one learns best from experienced others in the course of addressing real problems. But it is also true and that is where the self-conscious philanthropic act of mentoring comes into play. Mentoring is a gift unrewarded by an expectation of mutual reciprocity, but instead as a form of serial reciprocity, repaying the gift that one has been given by previous generations to pass on to those generations that follow. To raise that philanthropic act to consciousness, so as to be more deliberate and efficacious about it, would be one aspect of the mutual relationship between nursing and philanthropy.

Likewise with volunteers. As among the chief stewards of that resource in health care settings, nurses must self-consciously seek to enlarge the knowledge base of volunteers, to ensure that they are well used, and that their motivation is sustained. To treat volunteers as if they were part of the problem rather than being part of the solution is to endanger a philanthropic partnership that will grow in importance as the values of the marketplace become more dominant.

STATUS OF PHILANTHROPY AND NURSING IN THE
EDUCATION OF NURSES AND IN PROFESSIONAL DISCOURSE

Where and how do these roles get identified in the education—both formal and lifelong—of nurses? I would contend as a recent observer that they are virtually ignored. Take formal education as an example. At both the baccalaureate and graduate levels at a wide range of institutions, there are only two core courses— variously called "Health and Society," "Nursing as a Profession," "Policy and Practice Perspectives for Nursing" and "Legal and Ethical Aspects of Nursing"—where some of the issues might be raised, and from catalogue descriptions there is little evidence that that is the case. It is unlikely that they would be found in the required social science and ethics courses. With the possible exception of Community Nursing, these issues do not seem to enter the electives or cores of other specializations. Moreover, there do not seem to be electives that might include them. From statements of purpose and lists of competencies that ennoble all catalogues, the responsibility for mentoring and sustaining volunteers does not ever appear, and the civil roles of nursing must be inferred at a high level of abstraction. Nurses as part of the philanthropic team for fundraising or as donors, needless to say, appears nowhere.

This can be seen in the formative texts used in nursing. If we take the magisterial work of Virginia Henderson, especially the sixth edition of *Principles and Practice of Nursing*, we find a whole chapter devoted to "Nursing in the Social Order," but references to the civil society contributions of nurses limited to a few paragraphs in a text of 2,119 pages. Philanthropic values of trust and generosity are not touched on at all, except in relation to Florence Nightingale. Volunteers receive a paragraph, mentoring appears nowhere, and the peculiar characteristics of nonprofit, philanthropic health care work settings are never mentioned.

A more contemporary standard text, *Fundamentals of Nursing*, gives two pages to the history of nursing out of 1,540 pages, including the obligatory paragraph on Clara Barton, Margaret Sanger, and Lillian Wald and their contributions to our common agenda. Four times the space is given to various proponents of nursing theory. No mention is made of nonprofit, philanthropic work settings. Mentoring is not included in the chapters on communication and professional development. Volunteer agency appears in the index as the only reference to volunteering, between value-oriented spirometry and vomiting. Anything smacking of civil society and political engagement is exhausted by a reference to N-CAP and the judgment that "because they are not politically astute, nurses lack the political education to successfully compete in politics."

Another perspective is to see what is considered as "political" in a preparatory text for nurses. As we have discussed earlier, nurses are in a variety of settings where they are capable of helping to shape the common agenda—professional associations, service clubs, churches, volunteer activities, etc. They also bring important skills to discussions about values. In what appears to be the only book on the civil life of nurses, *The Politics of Nursing* by Beatrice and Philip Kalisch, the contention that nurses are politically naive and unable to make coalitions is repeated. The entire civil arena is seen as party politics and legislative action, and the proper understanding of the civil role of nurses is as an "interest group." This is, I believe, a partial view and fails to see the many civil roles nurses play. What nurses advocate is not always in their interest.

Finally, to what extent do the roles I have labeled as philanthropic appear in the nursing literature available to leaders and practitioners alike? Using the *Cumulative Index to Nursing and Allied Health Literature* (CINAHL), a database representing 560 journals from 1982 to the present with over 300,000 records, I ran various searches using concepts associated with philanthropy. Whether the key words were advocacy in social reform, managing volunteers, mentoring, or philanthropy itself, the aggregate number of hits was less than one thousandth of one percent of the database. The references that constituted "hits" were more often than not in journals with only local reach or in foreign periodicals. To say that the subject matter has been ignored may be an understatement.

What Might Be Done?

If the argument has been convincing, several steps could be taken to remedy the situation. First, professional associations and their student affiliates can become more self-conscious in their responsibilities as academies for participation in civil society, spending more time on thinking about the common health care agenda and designing ways to prepare their members to inform the public about it. Second, future editions of formative textbooks might include material on distinguishing characteristics of nonprofit health care, civil roles of nurses, the strategic importance of nurses in managing volunteers, the obligation of mentoring in furthering professional development, and the opportunities for philanthropic fundraising and gift-giving. The proceedings of this conference might be a starting point. An organization like Sigma Theta Tau might commission such a module. Third, leadership seminars might be held on such themes as "A Common Health Care Agenda Beyond Professions," "Advancing Civil Society" and "Philanthropic Initiatives in Health Care," with a view to strengthening the consciousness of nurses of the civil and philanthropic importance of their work. Fourth, the history of the contributions of nurses and nursing to American civil society—to shaping and advancing a common agenda—needs to be written. It can become a primer for the emerging agenda and a model for other professions. Finally, at least on a trial basis, a relationship between nursing and philanthropic studies—in teaching, continuing education and scholarship—should be entertained. May we begin yesterday.

OTHER BOOKS AVAILABLE FROM
SIGMA THETA TAU INTERNATIONAL

📖 *The Adventurous Years: Leaders in Action 1973-1999,* Henderson, 1998.

📖 *As We See Ourselves: Jewish Women in Nursing,* Benson, 2001.

📖 *Building and Managing a Career in Nursing: Strategies for Advancing Your Career,* Miller, 2003.

📖 *Cadet Nurse Stories: The Call for and Response of Women During World War II,* Perry and Robinson, 2001.

📖 *Collaboration for the Promotion of Nursing,* Briggs, Merk and Mitchell, 2003.

📖 *The Communication of Caring in Nursing,* Knowlden, 1998.

📖 *Creating Responsive Solutions to Healthcare Change,* McCullough, 2001.

📖 *Gerontological Nursing Issues for the 21st Century,* Gueldner and Poon, 1999.

📖 *The HeART of Nursing: Expressions of Creative Art in Nursing,* Wendler, 2002.

📖 *Immigrant Women and Their Health: An Olive Paper,* Ibrahim Meleis, Lipson, Muecke and Smith, 1998.

📖 *The Language of Nursing Theory and Metatheory,* King and Fawcett, 1997.

📖 *Making a Difference: Stories from the Point of Care,* Hudacek, 2000.

📖 *The Neuman Systems Model and Nursing Education: Teaching Strategies and Outcomes,* Lowry, 1998.

📖 *Nurses' Moral Practice: Investing and Discounting Self,* Kelly 2000.

📖 *Nursing and Philanthropy: An Energizing Metaphor for the 21st Century,* McBride, 2000.

📖 *The Roy Adaption Model-Based Research: 25 Years of Contributions fo Nursing Science,* Boston Based Adaption Research in Nursing Society, 1999.

📖 *Stories of Family Caregiving: Reconsideration of Theory, Literature, and Life,* Poirer and Ayres, 2002.

📖 *Virginia Avenel Henderson: Signature for Nursing,* Hermann, 1997

Call toll-free 1.888.634.7575 (U.S. and Canada) or
+800.634.7575.1 (International), or visit our Web site at
www.nursingsociety.org/publications for more information

Printed in the United States
1121500003B/112-576

9 781930 538023